Tessa Kiros

FOOD FROM MANY GREEK KITCHENS

Published in 2010 by Murdoch Books Pty Ltd

Murdoch Books Pty Limited Australia
Pier 8/9, 23 Hickson Road, Millers Point NSW 2000
Phone: +61 (0)2 8220 2000 Fax: +61 (0)2 8220 2558
www.murdochbooks.com.au

Murdoch Books UK Limited
Erico House, 6th Floor, 93–99 Upper Richmond Road, Putney, London SW15 2TG
Phone: +44 (0)20 8785 5995 Fax: +44 (0)20 8785 5985
www.murdochbooks.co.uk

Publisher: Kay Scarlett
Photography: Manos Chatzikonstantis
Illustrations & styling: Michail Touros
Art direction & design: Lisa Greenberg
Editor: Daniela Bertollo
Food Editor: Jo Glynn
Designer: Clare O'Loughlin
Production: Joan Beal

National Library of Australia Cataloguing-in-Publication Data
Kiros, Tessa. Greece/Tessa Kiros.
Includes index. ISBN 978174-1966848 (hbk.)
Cookery, Greek.
Dewey Number: 641.59495

PRINTED IN CHINA.
Colour reproduction by Splitting Image Colour Studio, Melbourne, Australia.

COOKING NOTES: You may find cooking times vary depending on the oven you are using.
For fan-forced ovens, as a general rule, set the oven temperature to 20°C (35°F) lower than
indicated in the recipe.

Tessa Kiros

FOOD FROM MANY GREEK KITCHENS

MURDOCH BOOKS

FOR GREECE
*May your ancient
Gods and Goddesses watch
over you always*

Aa

(alfa) is for Artemis, goddess of the hunt and of the moon. And Athena, the goddess of Athens, who gave her name to the capital of Greece. For Achilleas – the 'invincible' Trojan War hero with the vulnerable heel. Anithos (dill) – much used in greek dishes. Arni – lamb. And agapi – love.

Bb

(vita) like vassilopitta – the cake with the coin that brings in the new year. Also for vasilias – king, and vasilissa – queen.

Γγ

(yamma) like yiaourti (yoghurt) that in Greece needs no introduction. Partnered with savoury foods, or as a dessert with honey and nuts can't be bettered. Also for yelio – laughter.

Δδ

(delta) for Dionyssos – the god of wine and ylenti (good times, party). Or diosmos – mint, a nice surprise here and there in Greek cooking. And daphne – bay leaves – used regularly. Also for Delphi – the place where the most famous ancient oracle was housed.

Eε

(epsilon) is for elies – olives, ellines – Greeks and their wonderful spirit. Efcharisto – thanks, and Eros – the god of love.

Ζζ

(zita) as in zeimbekiko, the Greek dance that no-one can teach you. Dance it when you are blue. It is said that 'to learn zeimbekiko, you have to have loved, been hurt, cried and suffered first. Then it comes to you.' Also for zoi – life, zoo – animal and zachari – sugar.

Ηη

(ita) as in Hera, the goddess of family and Dias' (Zeus') wife. Also for Helios ... so much sun and warmth that people are led to Greece for:

Θη

(theta) as in Thalassa – the sea and so very very much of it that has shaped Greece's past and present. Also for thimari – thyme.

Ιι

(yiota) Ippocrates – the father of medicine. Ithaki – Odysseus' much longed for island and final destination.

Κκ

(kappa) Karavi – boat. Or kaiki (caique) – the traditional Greek boat. that can safely sway right down on its side and then bounce right back with the waves. Kyrie Eleison (Lord have mercy). Krassi – wine. And for the city of Kalamata with its wonderful olives.

Λλ

(lamda) for lambada the natural wax candle. Lagana – the bread eaten just before Easter. And for limani (port) and the laiki agora (street market selling fresh produce).

Μμ

(mi) is for Mykonos and Minos the ancient king of Crete. Mycenae (one of Greece's ancient kingdoms ruled by King Agamemnon). And Mani on the mainland of the Peloponnese. Also for Mati – the eye intended as the evil eye. Meli – which is honey. And the great actress Melina Mercouri.

Nν

(ni) as in Nissi – island. Hundreds of nissia. And nero – water.

Ξξ

(xi) Xenos – foreigner/stranger. Xigala a lovely soft slightly sour cheese from Crete – eaten with bread as a starter. Xidi (vinegar) and Xifias (swordfish).

Οο

(omikron) as in Olympus the mount of the gods. And Homer's Odyssey. The Olympic games which started in Greece's ancient city of Olympia. In Greek the 'o' and a 'u' together make a U sound as in ouzo.

Ππ

(pi) as in the Parthenon – the temple of Athena on the Acropolis. And for periptero – the many handy small, always open kiosks on the side of roads in Greece that sell everything. For the lovely island of Patmos ... where it is said that John received the apocalypse or revelation. And for Poseidon – god of the sea.

Ρρ

(ro) as in revithia – chickpeas. And raki – the strong Cretan digestive spirit.

Σσ

(sigma) as in Smyrni in Asia Minor (now Izmir in Turkey). It was inhabited by thousands of Greeks who were then evicted by the Turks in 1922. Some influences remain in dishes such as soutzoukakia (meatballs in tomato with cumin).

Tτ

(taf) is for tiropita – cheese pie. Trapezi – table, and tavli – backgammon (a national pastime in Greece). And for taverna – a traditional Greek restaurant.

Yυ

(ipsilon) as in Hydra the beautiful car-free island. Hypervoli (exaggeration). Hyperifanos (proud). And for Hygia (health)

Φφ

(fi) as in filia (friendship). Fotia (fire). Feggari (the moon). Fistikia – pistachio nuts – that the island of Aegina is so well known for.

Xχ

(xi) the island of Xios (Chios) and its wonderful masticha – a resin from the masticha trees used as an ingredient in some traditional ice creams, and in some breads like tsoureki.

Ψψ

(psi) as in psomi – bread, or psomaki – small breads (the much used diminutive in the Greek language). Psari – fish from the abundant waters, and psaras – fisherman. Psachno – to search, and psychi – soul.

Ωω

(omega) as in 'the alpha and omega of it all'.

CONTENTS

GLOSSARY

A

ALATOPIPERIGANO
seasoning made from
salt, black pepper and
dried oregano.

ANTHONERO
flower petal water.

ANTHOTIRO
a soft white creamy cheese,
similar to ricotta.

AVGOLEMONO
made from lemon juice and
beaten egg, widely used to
thicken soups and for sauces.

B

BAKALIAROS
salt cod that needs to be
soaked in fresh water for
several days to soften the
flesh and remove the salt.

BRIKI
long-handled coffee pot which
comes in different sizes and
made from various metals
such as copper, stainless
steel and aluminium.

C

CAPER LEAVES
pickled caper sprigs with
leaves are available in jars
from Greek delicatessens.

CELERY
Greek celery is thinner and
smaller than regular celery
and is stronger in flavour.
It has lovely green stalks
and leaves – both are used
in cooking.

CHORTA
also spelt horta. Wild leafy
greens found everywhere
in Greece.

F

FAVA
name of the dish usually
made with dried yellow
split peas and sometimes
yellow lentils or dried yellow
broad beans.

FETA CHEESE
most commonly made now
using cow's milk, but also
still made with sheep's or
goat's milk.

FLORINIS
small sweet red peppers
from the Florina region in
Greece. Lovely roasted.

FRIGANIES
dried bread cut into
thin slices.

G

GLISTRIDA
Greek for purslane. Used
fresh in salads or cooked
as you would spinach. also
known as andrakla.

GRATING
Grating onions and tomatoes
gives a fine soft texture
without puréeing them.

GREEK YOGHURT
thicker and creamier
than regular yoghurts.

H

HILOPITES
rough-cut squares of noodles/
pasta, often homemade but
can be bought dried.

HORIATIKI
also spelt choriatiki, is the
traditional Greek salad.

K

KAIMAKI
ice cream often flavoured
with masticha and sometimes
with salepi.

KALAMAKI
literally, 'little reed'.
These are the wooden
skewers or also refer to
the souvlaki proper.

KASSERI
medium-hard sheep's milk
cheese similar to pecorino.

KRITHARAKI
orzo or rice-shaped
dried pasta.

L

LADOLEMONO
a sauce or dressing made
with lemon juice and oil.

M

MASTICHA
also spelt mastic, is tree resin
used for flavouring as well
as for its gum properties.

MEZE
small dishes or appetisers
to be shared.

MIZITHRA
an almost sweet, hard white
cheese often grated over
cooked dishes. Can also be
soft like ricotta.

OKRA
also known as lady's
fingers, this mucilaginous
plant is greatly appreciated
in cooking.

OREGANO
used dried in Greek
cooking. If possible,
buy bunches imported
from Greece (wrapped in
cellophane) from
Greek delis.

OUZO
the popular, licorice-flavoured
apéritif that magically
changes colour when water or
ice is added.

PHYLLO PASTRY
also spelt filo. Different
manufacturers make sheets
of different dimensions
and thicknesses.

RAKI
also called tsikoudia, it is
a clear spirit.

RICE
a medium-grain rice,
called Karolina, is most
often used in Greece for
stuffing or dolmades.

SAGANAKI
little single-serve frying pans.
The most popular saganaki is
made with slices of a cheese
such as kefalotiri, kasseri and
sheep's milk feta.

SALEPI
also spelt sahlepi.
A flavouring made from
the ground roots of wild
orchids.

SIKOTARIA
lamb intestines used in the
traditional Easter soup.

TAPSI
a baking dish, usually metal,
with low sides. Most Greek
housewives have a number of
different sizes and shapes.

TARAMA
also spelt taramas, it's salted
and cured roe of cod, grey
mullet or carp.

TRAHANA
also spelt trachanas: cracked
wheat mixed with yoghurt and
then dried.

TRADITIONAL

FOODS

for eg ... tradition goes that vassilopitta is what you will eat in the New Year. Everyone has a vassilopitta at New Year. Even in many schools, each class gets one. And the truly wonderful thing about this cake is that a flouri (coin) is dropped in before baking. The idea is that no-one knows where the coin is. Before serving, slices are cut and named – one for the Virgin Mary, one for Christ, one for the poor, one for the household, and then from the oldest member of the family or friends present, each gets a piece. The nominated pieces are then distributed, and if you are the lucky one to have the coin hidden in your piece of cake, you will be blessed for the whole year. Don't you love that sense of celebration and tradition the Greeks have?

VASSILOPITTA NEW YEAR WISH CAKE

Βασιλόπιτα

MAKES 1 BIG CAKE

1 COIN SUCH AS A EURO, DOLLAR OR POUND

450 G (1 LB/3 CUPS) PLAIN (ALL-PURPOSE) FLOUR

3 HEAPED TEASPOONS BAKING POWDER

200 G (7 OZ) UNSALTED BUTTER, ROOM TEMPERATURE

300 G (10½ OZ) SUGAR

4 EGGS

1 TEASPOON VANILLA EXTRACT

1 TABLESPOON GRATED ORANGE ZEST

1 TABLESPOON GRATED LEMON ZEST

4 TABLESPOONS BRANDY

185 ML (6 FL OZ/¾ CUP) MILK

50 G (1¾ OZ/⅓ CUP) BLANCHED ALMONDS, FINELY CHOPPED

ICING (CONFECTIONERS') SUGAR, FOR DUSTING

You may find different versions of the vassilopitta, from a regular cake like this one to a yeasted bread with different spices in. If you don't bake the cake with the flouri (coin) in, once it's baked you can turn the cake over and push a sharp knife into a selected spot, making a thin slit about 3 cm (1¼ inches) deep. Insert the flouri into the slit, then turn the cake back to the right way up so nobody can tell where the coin is.

Preheat the oven to 180°c (350°f/gas 4). Butter and flour a 28 cm (11¼ inch) spring-form cake tin. Rinse the coin, dry it well and wrap it tightly in aluminium foil. Sift the flour, baking powder and a pinch of salt together into a bowl.

Whip the butter and sugar together with electric beaters in a large bowl until creamy. Add the eggs one at a time, whisking each one in well. Beat in the vanilla and the orange and lemon zests. Fold in the dry ingredients alternately with the brandy and the milk, then fold the almonds in. Scrape into the tin. Drop in the coin now, trying to keep it upright, not flat. Bake for 50 to 60 minutes or until a skewer inserted into the centre comes out clean. Cool in the tin for 5 minutes before turning out onto a wire cake rack to cool completely.

Put a doily on top of the cake and dust with icing sugar before removing it to reveal a lacy pattern. You can also cut a stencil of the numbers of the year you are in (eg 1949) and dust that. Cut a piece for everybody and serve.

YAMOPILAFO WEDDING RICE

Γαμοπίλαφο

SERVES 4 OR SO

1 SMALL SHOULDER OF LAMB (ABOUT 600 G/1 LB 5 OZ), CUT INTO 2–3 PIECES, THROUGH THE BONE, BY YOUR BUTCHER

3 TABLESPOONS OLIVE OIL

2 WHITE ONIONS (180 G/ 6½ OZ), FINELY CHOPPED

1 BAY LEAF

2 GARLIC CLOVES, FINELY CHOPPED

1 TEASPOON GROUND CINNAMON

125 ML (4 FL OZ/½ CUP) WHITE WINE

250 G (9 OZ) MEDIUM-GRAIN RICE

20 G (¾ OZ) BUTTER

COARSELY GRATED ANTHOTIRO, FIRM MIZITHRA OR SALTED RICOTTA, TO SERVE

SMALL HANDFUL COARSELY CHOPPED FLAT-LEAF PARSLEY, TO SERVE

Most probably you will have more than four guests for this occasion (which is what this recipe serves), but it is easy to increase these amounts.

The lamb can be served separately as a second course if you like. Also, you can add a chicken for depth in flavour as they do in Crete, which is where this dish is from.

Traditionally staka (a butter made from goat's milk) is added. All this richness should cut through the raki and various wines drunk at the wedding celebration. The next morning (a taxi driver told me), after dancing all night, a mug of rooster broth is had by all the party animals, along with a plate of hilopites (noodles) with coarsely grated mizithra over the top. This should settle the stomach and give one new energy for the day just dawned.

Rinse the lamb and wipe it all over with a damp cloth. Pat dry. Heat the oil in a heavy-based pot which has a lid and fry the skin side of the lamb pieces until golden brown. Turn them over and when the new underside is starting to brown, add the onion and bay leaf around the sides. Fry them, stirring, until golden, along with the lamb. Add the garlic to the onion and sprinkle the cinnamon and some salt and pepper over the lamb. Stir through and cook until the garlic starts to smell good, then stir the wine through. When most of it has evaporated add 500 ml (17 fl oz/ 2 cups) of hot water. Bring to the boil, cover with a lid and simmer for 1 hour. Add another 250 ml (9 fl oz/1 cup) of water, turn the lamb *over and simmer for about 30 minutes more, turning once or twice, or until the meat is falling off the bone. Remove the lamb and keep it warm and covered. Stir the rice into the pot and add 1 litre (35 fl oz/4 cups) of hot water. Simmer, covered, until most of the liquid has been absorbed, about 20 minutes. Season with salt.*

When the rice is almost ready, remove the lamb bones and shred the meat. Add the butter to the rice and turn through. Serve the rice in bowls with some shredded lamb on top, a scattering of cheese and then parsley and a grind of pepper.

OPA!

AN EXCLAMATION USED WHEN SINGING OR DANCING ...

BAKLAVADAKIA SMALL BAKLAVA

Μπακλαβαδάκια

MAKES 56

ABOUT 170 G (6 OZ) BUTTER

ABOUT 550 G (1 LB 4 OZ) PHYLLO PASTRY, EG 13 SHEETS OF 48 X 37 CM (19 X 14½ INCHES)

200 G (7 OZ) SHELLED UNSALTED PISTACHIO NUTS

SYRUP

180 G (6½ OZ) SUGAR

4½ TABLESPOONS MILD RUNNY HONEY

These are my favourite baklava. Individual small ones packed row by row into a large tray. It's quite easy and totally worth it when you get your head around the maths. It may even give you a wonderful sense of achievement when they come out of the oven. The dish size, 26 x 30 cm (10 x 12 inches) with straight sides, is important to give you 8 rows of 7 baklava – (56 baklava). If your dish size is different, you may have to adjust the amount of baklava for a packed-in result full of rows and rows of baklava. Also, the dimensions and weight of commercial phyllo varies from brand to brand and so you might need some additional maths to work out the number of sheets to use.

To make the syrup, stir the sugar and honey with 275 ml (9½ fl oz) of water in a saucepan until the sugar dissolves, then bring to the boil. Simmer for about 10 minutes or until slightly thickened. Cool.

Preheat the oven to 180°c (350°f/gas 4). Melt the butter in a small saucepan until pale golden and smelling great. Cover the phyllo sheets with a clean dry cloth to stop them drying out while you work. Spread one sheet of phyllo on your work surface. Brush gently but well and generously all over with butter. Cover with the next sheet of phyllo, brush with butter and continue in this way until you have a stack of 6 sheets. Using a ruler and a sharp knife, measure and cut 7 cm (2¾ inch) squares. Fill and form this batch before buttering the next so that the phyllo won't dry.

Working quickly, drop about 4 pistachios into the centre of each square. Bring the four sides together to form a boat, then pinch them together at about two-thirds of the way up so the points of the phyllo open out like petals. Don't squash the top leaves together as their layerings are important for look and taste. Make sure that the bases are kept as square as possible, and they should measure about 3 cm (1¼ inches) square.

Brush the base and sides of a 26 x 30 cm (10½ x 12 inch) ovenproof dish with melted butter. Line up the baklava in neat compact rows like bon-bons in a chocolate box. Repeat the full procedure with

another 6 sheets of phyllo and continue until you have made 56 baklava. If you are respecting the measures given here, you may need to fold and cut a single phyllo sheet to make up the last few. Flick a little cold water over them with your fingers. Bake for 25 to 30 minutes until crisp and pale golden.

Drizzle half the syrup evenly over the hot baklava in long thin drizzles. Chop the remaining pistachios finely and scatter some over each baklava. Drizzle over the rest of the syrup to hold the nuts in place. Cool before serving. Keep, unrefrigerated, in the dish in which it's made covered by a cake net, or in a leakproof cake box of the type that you'd get from the baker's.

BAKLAVA

Μπακλαβάς

MAKES ABOUT 30

150 G (5½ OZ) ALMONDS, CRUSHED, BUT WITH SOME TEXTURE

150 G (5½ OZ) WALNUTS, CRUSHED, BUT WITH SOME TEXTURE

2 TABLESPOONS SUGAR

2 TEASPOONS GROUND CINNAMON

22 SHEETS OF PHYLLO PASTRY* CUT TO THE DIMENSIONS OF YOUR DISH

ABOUT 150 G (5½ OZ) UNSALTED BUTTER, MELTED TO GOLDEN BROWN

30 OR SO WHOLE CLOVES, FOR DECORATING

SYRUP

360 G (12¾ OZ) SUGAR

2 TABLESPOONS HONEY

JUICE OF ½ LEMON

STRIP OF LEMON PEEL

2 OR 3 SMALL CINNAMON ROLLS

I love this Chanel bag looking thing. It is served, most often with a glass of water, throughout the year and at most celebrations, and on Sundays too. Working with phyllo may take a little getting used to. You need to work quickly so that the pastry doesn't dry out, and gently so that it doesn't tear. You may find it easier (at least for the first 10 layers) to put a layer onto your work surface, brush with butter, then put another layer of phyllo neatly over that, smoothing it down as you would the sheets of a bed that you were making. Repeat until all your layers are on, then the pile of sheets can be lowered into your dish.

Preheat the oven to 180°c (350°f/gas 4). To make the syrup, put the sugar, honey, lemon juice, lemon peel and cinnamon in a saucepan with 1 cup water and bring to the boil, stirring. Simmer for 5 to 6 minutes then take off the heat and cool.

Mix the almonds, walnuts, sugar and cinnamon together in a bowl. Have the phyllo sheets ready, covered by a tea towel to prevent them drying out. Brush the base of a 22 x 30 cm (8½ x 12 inch) ovenproof dish with butter. Lay 1 sheet of phyllo on the bottom and brush with butter. Cover with another sheet, brush it with butter and continue in this way until you have a neat stack of 10 sheets lining the bottom of the dish. Spread half the nut mixture over the phyllo, patting it down firmly and levelling the surface. Cover with another

*2 sheets of phyllo, buttering each
one. Scatter the rest of the nuts over
evenly and press down gently. Now
lay down the last 10 sheets of phyllo,
buttering each one of course and
finishing with the last layer buttered.*

*Using a small sharp knife, cut
diamonds on the diagonal of about
6 x 6 cm (2½ x 2½ inch). Cut
all the way through the layers of
phyllo as this will make it easier
to lift out the pieces when serving.
Flick just a little cold water over
the top to prevent the layers from
curling up. Stud the centre of each
diamond with a clove. Bake for 25
to 30 minutes or until gently golden
on top. Gently pour half the syrup
all over the baklava. Wait for it to
be absorbed then pour over the rest.
Leave to cool totally before serving.*

*Will keep, unrefrigerated, for at least
a week, covered with a tea towel or
net to deter bees and flies.*

✤ *The dimensions of commercial
phyllo changes from brand to brand,
so you will need to work out the
number of phyllo sheets you require
in the beginning, according to the
maker's dimensions.*

DIPLES
FRIED FOLDS

Δίπλες

MAKES: MANY, MANY

6 EGGS, SEPARATED

½ TEASPOON BAKING
POWDER

500 G (1 LB 2 OZ/3⅓ CUPS)
PLAIN (ALL-PURPOSE)
FLOUR

1 TEASPOON VANILLA
EXTRACT

1 TABLESPOON OLIVE OIL

LIGHT OLIVE OIL,
FOR FRYING

1 TEASPOON GROUND
CINNAMON, TO DUST

¼ TEASPOON GROUND
CLOVES, TO DUST

20 G (¾ OZ) WALNUTS,
FINELY CHOPPED

SYRUP

700 G (1 LB 9 OZ/2 CUPS)
MILD HONEY

1 HEAPED TABLESPOON
SUGAR

3 TEASPOONS LEMON JUICE

These are rather celebrational, the kind of thing you'd serve on a name day, or take to someone's house for a special event.

This is Roulla's recipe. She showed us how to make them at her house and it felt like we were preparing for a wedding or 20 name days, we made so many. The rolling and shaping in the pan is not so easy, you may need a few tries before you get the hang of it. The honey to use is important – what you use is what you will find on your plate – so not too strong is best. Roulla used a mild wild thyme honey. Some people leave out the walnuts on top, others sprinkle on some sesame seeds.

These will keep for a few days, preferably covered with a cake net. This makes a huge amount, so if you like you can even try half a dose.

Whisk the egg whites with electric beaters until creamy and fluffy. Add the yolks and continue beating for 20 or 30 seconds to reduce the egginess. Transfer to a large bowl, add the baking powder and start adding the flour, mixing it first with a wooden spoon then changing to your hands as it gets stiffer. Add flour until you have a soft, non-sticky dough. Add the vanilla and knead it in. Lastly add the olive oil and knead until you have a smooth, soft dough. Mark a cross on the top with the edge of your hand, cover the bowl with a tea towel and leave at room temperature for 30 minutes or so.

Divide the dough in half. Scatter some flour onto a large work surface. Stretch one piece of dough and start flattening it with your hands. Take over with a rolling pin and roll it as *thinly as possible to a rough oval about 70 x 46 cm (27½ x 18 inches). Cut 12 cm (4½ inch) wide long strips, then cut in the opposite direction to give lengths of 9 cm (3½ inches). Once cut, these can be rolled or stretched with your hands to 15 x 12 cm (6 x 4½ inches). Lay, not touching, on a couple of tea towels and cover with more tea towels to prevent them drying out. Repeat the rolling and cutting with the second half of the dough.*

Pour oil into a large non-stick frying pan to a depth of 2 cm (¾ inch) and put over medium–high heat. Lay the first dough rectangle in the oil. With a fork in each hand, press down on each end of the dough to prevent it turning up. Then with one fork grab the middle of the dough from underneath

and flip it so it folds once on itself then roll it with the fork in the middle as though you were rolling a forkful of spaghetti. Fry until crisp and golden, about 20 seconds, holding it to keep its shape and turning it over if necessary. Using the forks, lift it from the oil and tilt it over the pan for a couple of seconds to drain off excess oil. Place it on a tray lined with paper towels. Fry the rest of the dough strips in this way, stacking them in a large dish once they have drained. Reduce the oil temperature if it becomes too hot at any time.

For the syrup, put the honey in a wide pot and add the sugar and 100 ml (3½ fl oz) of water. Bring slowly to the boil and as soon as it reaches boiling point, remove it from the heat. Add the lemon juice. Drop

continued

in the diples, one at a time and leave for 30 seconds or so to drink in the honey. Turn over, leave a bit longer and then lift out with your 2 forks, tilting it to drain off excess honey. Stack them in a large roasting dish and once you have a full layer, lightly dust the tops with cinnamon. Turn them over and dust the other side, this time with just a hint of cloves as well. Sprinkle the tops lightly with walnuts then continue dipping, layering and dusting. When you have finished you may feel surprised that you have made these. I would suggest that you make them the day before you want to serve them so that you are not all hot and flustered, with a kitchen that needs cleaning just before people arrive.

Name days are given a lot of importance in Greece – it seems easier for some to remember a name than a date of birth? And then anyway all the Nikos can celebrate together one day, the Marias another and some overlap like St. Constantine and St. Helen are on the same day ... (and so there can be much celebration together).

FANOUROPITA CAKE FOR LOST THINGS

Φανουρόπιτα

MAKES 1 CAKE

360 G (12¾ OZ) PLAIN
(ALL-PURPOSE) FLOUR

1 TABLESPOON BAKING
POWDER

160 G (5¾ OZ) SUGAR

1 TEASPOON GROUND
CINNAMON

185 ML (6 FL OZ/¾ CUP)
LIGHT OLIVE OIL

185 ML (6 FL OZ/¾ CUP)
FRESH ORANGE JUICE

1 TEASPOON VANILLA
EXTRACT

This simple, easy to whip together cake is made in honour of St. Fanourios, the patron saint of lost things. The day before St. Fanourios day, one can imagine the scent of cakes baking filling kitchens everywhere. They are taken to church the following day where they are blessed and then shared out among the people. A fanouropita can be made any time of year though – when something is lost such as a ring, or a lover or even when a mind is in search of an answer. The cake is ideal during the fasting period as it has no eggs and no butter.

Preheat the oven to 190°c (375°f/ gas 5). Brush a 24 cm (9½ inch) spring-form tin with oil, and flour it. In a bowl stir the flour, baking powder, sugar and cinnamon together. Add the olive oil, orange juice and vanilla and whisk with electric beaters until combined. It will be very thick. Scrape into your tin and bake until a skewer inserted into the centre comes out clean, about 40 minutes. Cool on a wire cake rack before cutting and distributing appropriately. Keeps well for 5 or 6 days in an airtight container.

KOURABIEDES BUTTERY ALMOND CAKES

Κουραμπιέδες

MAKES ABOUT 22

50 G (1¾ OZ/⅓ CUP) ALMONDS, SKIN ON

250 G (9 OZ) UNSALTED BUTTER, ROOM TEMPERATURE

2 TABLESPOONS ICING (CONFECTIONERS') SUGAR

1 EGG YOLK

1 TEASPOON VANILLA ESSENCE

1 TABLESPOON BRANDY

300 G (10½ OZ/2 CUPS) PLAIN (ALL-PURPOSE) FLOUR

1 TEASPOON BAKING POWDER

ABOUT 250 G (9 OZ/2 CUPS) ICING (CONFECTIONERS') SUGAR, FOR DUSTING

These are icing sugary/buttery, and melt-in-your-mouth honest bundles enjoyed at Christmas.

Coarsely chop the almonds into small pieces. Toast in a dry frying pan over a low-ish heat until just coloured. Cool.

Whisk the butter in a bowl using electric beaters until it is very pale and thick, about 8 minutes. Add the icing sugar and whisk it in well. Add the egg yolk, vanilla and brandy and whisk them in well too. Sift in the flour and baking powder and beat them in until you have a smooth dough which is hard to keep mixing with the beaters. Add the almonds and mix them through with your hands. Press the dough into a ball, cover with plastic wrap and refrigerate for 30 to 40 minutes.

Meanwhile, preheat the oven to 180°c (350°f/gas 4) and line a baking tray with baking paper. Break off pieces of dough, about 30 g (1¼ oz) each, and roll them into balls, slightly flattening the tops. Put them on the tray allowing a little space between each one. Bake until lightly golden, 20 to 25 minutes. Remove from the oven and let cool on the tray for about 15 minutes.

Dust about half of the icing sugar onto a tray or large plate or your tin where you will store them. Gently move the kourabiedes to sit in a single layer in this, then sprinkle the remaining icing sugar over their tops so that they look like they are snowed in. Will keep in a tin for many days.

MELOMAKARONA HONEY CAKES

Μελομακάρονα

MAKES 15

70 G (2½ OZ) SUGAR

185 ML (6 FL OZ/¾ CUP) EXTRA VIRGIN OLIVE OIL

3 TABLESPOONS BRANDY

JUICE OF ½ ORANGE

1 TEASPOON GRATED ORANGE ZEST

1 TEASPOON BAKING POWDER

½ TEASPOON BAKING SODA

2 TEASPOONS GROUND CINNAMON

¼ TEASPOON GROUND CLOVES

¼ TEASPOON GRATED NUTMEG

300 G (10½ OZ/2 CUPS) PLAIN (ALL-PURPOSE) FLOUR

15 WHOLE CLOVES

20 G (¾ OZ) CRUSHED WALNUTS, TO SERVE

SYRUP

½ CUP HONEY

140 G (5 OZ) SUGAR

1 STRIP ORANGE ZEST

1 SMALL CINNAMON ROLL

This is Katerina's wonderful recipe. Katerina is Irini's cousin. Irini is our photographer Manos' girlfriend. Melomakarona are small cakes drenched in honey syrup which shout 'Christmas' in Greece. Take them as gifts in a box, or eat them slowly throughout the season. You can make them smaller if you like, even half this size (which are truly lovely).

Preheat the oven to 180°c (350°f/gas 4) and line a baking tray with baking paper. Stir the sugar and oil in a wide bowl until dissolved. Add the brandy, orange juice and zest. Mix the baking powder, baking soda, ground cinnamon, ground cloves and nutmeg through the flour. Add to the bowl and mix to a loose dough with a wooden spoon. Using your hands, knead to a soft and smooth dough.

Break off small clumps of dough of about 40 g (1½ oz) each (you should get 15). Roll them into a ball between your palms then form small oval soaps of about 6 x 4 cm (2½ x 1½ inches). Set them onto the baking tray and bake until firm and the bases are gold, about 30 minutes.

While they are baking, make the syrup. Put all the ingredients along with 185 ml (6 fl oz/¾ cup) of water in a small pot and stir over medium heat until the sugar dissolves. Simmer for 5 minutes, then keep warm.

Put the cakes in a dish with sides where they will fit in one layer. Stud each with a clove. Pour the syrup over them, covering each well. Leave for 5 minutes. Spoon some syrup (it will be a little thicker now) from the bottom of the dish over the tops of the cakes and sprinkle with the walnuts. Remove to a serving plate. Drizzle the walnuts with remaining syrup. Cover with a cake net and cool completely. Will keep for many days, stored in a covered container.

TSIKNOPEMPTI

'Tsikna' is the smell of barbecuing meat and 'Pempti' is Thursday. So on this Thursday during carnival, about 1½ weeks before Clean Monday, you will find everyone eating grilled meat. Many people go out to eat in restaurants and to celebrate carnival out in the streets.

PAIDAKIA GRILLED LAMB CHOPS

Παϊδάκια

SERVES 3 TO 4

1 KG (2 LB 4 OZ) LAMB CHOPS (CUTLETS), UNTRIMMED

4 TABLESPOONS OLIVE OIL

JUICE OF 2 LEMONS

1 TEASPOON DRIED OREGANO

1 LARGE GARLIC CLOVE, PEELED AND SQUASHED

ALATOPIPERIGANO (PAGE 128), FOR SERVING

LEMON WEDGES, FOR SERVING

I love the way you can order these by the kilo (or half) in some grill places. On the table we always have a dish of tzatziki (page 130), fava (page 74) and a Greek salad (page 223). I also love tirokafteri (spicy feta, page 142) here. You should put some bread slices on the barbecue too, just after the meat, grill a bit, then remove to a plate and drizzle the slices with olive oil and scatter with the salt, pepper and crumbled oregano mix (alatopiperigano).

The lamb chops are best small with their fat left on – which is great grilled – but of course whoever doesn't like the fat can cut it away.

Rinse the chops if necessary, or wipe with a damp paper towel and put in a dish. Make the marinade in a bowl with the olive oil, lemon juice, oregano, garlic, about ½ teaspoon of salt and a few grinds of pepper. Splash about 4 tablespoons for now over the chops, cover with plastic wrap and leave for an hour or so.

Preheat the barbecue to hot. Put the chops on a grill rack about 10 cm (4 inches) from the coals and grill till deep brown and crusty looking here and there on both sides, but not dried out, basting often with the rest of the marinade. Remove to a platter, crumble a little of the alatopiperigano over and serve at once with the lemon wedges.

KATHARI DEFTERA – CLEAN MONDAY

Many people fly a kite on this day and most eat these: taramosalata, dolmades with no meat in the filling, lagana, taramokeftedes and halva. No meat is eaten. Picnics are taken out with these dishes and also vegetables, oysters and other seafood.

LAGANA ONCE-A-YEAR BREAD

Λαγάνα

MAKES 1 BREAD

14 G (½ OZ) FRESH YEAST, OR 2 TEASPOONS (7 G/¼ OZ) DRIED

PINCH OF SUGAR

400 G (14 OZ/2⅔ CUPS) BREAD (STRONG) FLOUR

½ TEASPOON SALT

4 TABLESPOONS OLIVE OIL

FOR THE TOP

1 TABLESPOON BREAD (STRONG) FLOUR

½ TABLESPOON OLIVE OIL

¼ TEASPOON SALT

1½ TABLESPOONS SESAME SEEDS

This is just a once-a-year bread in Greece, for the kite flying and taramokeftedes time. But of course you can make it as many times in the year as you like.

I got this recipe from an old baker in Mesolonghi, who described it as a flat bread with a puckered look on top. And the trick, he says, is the fluid flour and water mixture that gets brushed on before baking. And a good scattering of sesame seeds. Lagana is best eaten on the day made. If you want to make in advance, seal in a plastic bag and store in the freezer. You can double this amount here and make 2 loaves as it's always good to have on a day like Clean Monday. This bread makes great toasts (friganies) – cut up the next day and dry-grilled in the oven.

Crumble the fresh yeast or sprinkle the dried yeast into a large bowl. Add the sugar and 200 ml (7 fl oz) of lukewarm water and leave until it starts to activate and bubble. Add the flour, salt and olive oil and mix together with a wooden spoon until a loose dough forms. If it seems too dry, then add a few more drops of water. Knead for about 6 or 7 minutes on a lightly floured surface until the dough is smooth and spongy. Wipe out the bowl with an oiled paper towel and put the dough in. Cover the bowl with plastic wrap then a tea towel and leave in a warm spot for about 2½ hours or until puffed and doubled in size. Line a baking tray with baking paper. Knock the dough down and shape by stretching and rolling it into a rough rectangle of about 24 x 32 cm (9½ x 12¾ inches) and about 8 mm (⅜ inch) thick. Put onto the lined tray and dent many holes all over the surface with the tips of your fingers for a puckered look. Cover with tea towels and leave in the warm spot for 30 minutes or so to rise again.

Preheat the oven to 200°c (400°f/gas 6). For the top, whisk the flour, oil, salt and 2 tablespoons of water together. Gently brush all over the top of the bread, then sprinkle with the sesame seeds. Bake for about 20 minutes or until golden.

TARAMOSALATA

Ταραμοσαλάτα

MAKES JUST OVER 2 CUPS

2 OR 3 BIG SLICES OF
COUNTRY-STYLE BREAD
(ABOUT 100 G/3½ OZ),
WITHOUT CRUST

120 G (4½ OZ) TARAMA

PINCH OF PAPRIKA

½ RED ONION, PEELED AND
GRATED ON THE LARGE
HOLES OF A GRATER

325 ML (11 FL OZ) LIGHT
OLIVE OIL

JUICE OF 2–2½ LEMONS

This is most often served as a meze, a dip that would precede other dishes, or it stands beautifully among other seafood bits and pieces.

Tarama is salted cod or grey mullet roe and is a dusty rusty colour to start with. Mixed with the other ingredients its colour dilutes to an antique beige-pink. Some people do drop in some food colour to make it more pink which is how you might find it here and there. And some use potato instead of bread. Tarama is available in Greek supermarkets and delicatessens. Taramosalata is wonderful with breads such as lagana (page 50) or koulouria (page 161) and a dish of olives. At first it may taste a little strong, but give it a few hours in the fridge to soften. The next day is lovely. Taramosalata will keep well in the fridge, covered, for 2 to 3 days.

Tear up the bread into a bowl. Splash with a little water, just enough to dampen, and leave for a few minutes. Squeeze out all the water and put the bread back in the bowl. Add the tarama, paprika and the onion with its juice.

Whisk with electric beaters, adding a little of the oil as though you were making mayonnaise. Add a few drops of the lemon juice, beat in, then some oil and continue in this way until all the oil is in and you have enough lemon juice for your taste. Switch to a hand-held blender and pulse it to give a smooth consistency. If it seems too thick, pulse in a little water.

TARAMOKEFTEDES TARAMA BALLS

Ταραμοκεφτέδες

MAKES ABOUT 24

200 G (7 OZ) CRUSTLESS YESTERDAY'S BREAD

1 LARGE GARLIC CLOVE

70 G (2½ OZ) TARAMA

½ RED ONION, GRATED ON THE LARGE HOLES OF A GRATER

1 TEASPOON ROUGHLY CHOPPED MINT

1 TABLESPOON ROUGHLY CHOPPED FLAT-LEAF PARSLEY

1 TABLESPOON LEMON JUICE

PLAIN (ALL-PURPOSE) FLOUR, FOR DUSTING

LIGHT OLIVE OIL, FOR FRYING

1 LEMON, QUARTERED

For these fried tarama balls, you should use a good dense country bread, not the light airy type. These are best eaten on Clean Monday out on a picnic somewhere in the hills, if you want, make them in between flying kites.

This is a lovely meze with ouzo, that can mingle well with many dishes – and great, of course, to precede any fish or seafood dish.

Tear the bread into pieces, put in a bowl and splash with just enough water to dampen. Leave for a few minutes then squeeze it out over the sink until dry. Return the bread to the bowl. Crush the garlic with a pinch of salt into a paste using the flat of your knife, then add to the bread. Add the tarama, onion and its juice, mint, parsley and lemon juice, and a little pepper. Mix thoroughly with your hands. It shouldn't need salt, but taste to see. Shape into balls the size of a small cherry tomato (about 20 g/ ¾ oz). Leave to rest for 15 minutes or so.

Put some flour on a plate and roll the balls in it to cover them. Add the olive oil to a depth of about ½ cm (¼ inch) in a large non-stick frying pan and put over medium– high heat. Add the balls and fry until nicely golden all over, shaking the pan once or twice to make sure nothing is stuck. Remove with a slotted spoon and drain on a plate lined with paper towels. Sprinkle with a little salt. Eat warm, with a few drops of lemon juice.

DOLMADES STOVETOP STUFFED VINE LEAVES

Ντολμάδες στην κατσαρόλα

MAKES 35 TO 40

35–40 GOOD VINE LEAVES, PLUS A FEW TORN ONES

6 TABLESPOONS OLIVE OIL

2 RED ONIONS, GRATED ON THE LARGE HOLES OF A GRATER

200 G (7 OZ) MEDIUM-GRAIN RICE

3 LARGE TOMATOES, GRATED ON LARGE HOLES OF A GRATER (SO SKINS STAY BEHIND IN YOUR HAND), PLUS 1 EXTRA FOR THE TOPPING

½ CUP CHOPPED FLAT-LEAF PARSLEY

JUICE OF 1 LEMON

1 TEASPOON DRIED MINT

Bottled and pre-packed vine leaves are already blanched and are available from large supermarkets, Greek and Middle Eastern food stores.

To use fresh vine leaves, collect them from the last 20 cm (8 inches) or so of unsprayed young vines. Choose leaves which are roughly the size of your hand and which are tender, unmarked and not torn. Cut them off leaving just a few millimetres of the stem at the base of the leaf. Rinse and drain them twice. Put in stacks of 20 or so, then roll them up into a loose cigar and tie with string. Dip each roll into a pot of boiling water; just in and out, then drain and cool. If you are not going to use them straight away, put the rolls in an airtight container and freeze.

This is a lovely, traditional, no-meat version of dolmades, suitable for the fasting period before Easter. These are great with tzatziki (page 130) and are good served warm or at room temperature. Some even love them cold.

Before wrapping up the filling in the leaves, I like to weigh the filling and divide it by the amount of leaves. Less precisely, but still a good idea, is to divide the mixture into quarters so it's easier to visualise how you are travelling amount-wise.

If using bought leaves, put them in a large bowl of cold water to soak for a few minutes. Drain, pat dry with paper towels then stack in piles for later. Heat 5 tablespoons of the oil in a large frying pan which has a lid and sauté the onion over medium heat until golden. Add the rice, stir until coated, then add the grated tomato, parsley, lemon juice and mint, and season well with salt and pepper. Put the lid on and simmer for about 10 minutes or until the rice has softened and plumped up, and most of the liquid has been absorbed. Remove from the heat and leave with the lid on for 5 minutes or so.

Use a few torn vine leaves to cover the bottom of a wide heavy-based pot. Lay a few whole vine leaves at a time on your work surface, shiny side down. Spoon a heaped tablespoon of filling (about 20 g/¾ oz) onto each leaf and roll it up neatly and quite snugly, tucking in the sides after the first roll and continuing to roll them. Put them in the pot in concentric circles, starting on the outside, and make a second layer if necessary. Grate (so that the skin stays behind in your hand) the remaining tomato over the top, pour in about 750 ml (26 fl oz/3 cups) of hot water or enough to cover and drizzle in the remaining oil. Season with a little salt. Put a snug-fitting upturned plate over the top to keep the dolmades submerged. Cover and bring to the boil. Lower the heat and simmer for about 1 hour until the dolmades are tender and much of the liquid has been absorbed. Turn off the heat and rest them for 10 minutes or so before serving.

DOLMADES BAKED STUFFED VINE LEAVES

Ντολμάδες στον φούρνο

MAKES 35 TO 40

35–40 GOOD VINE LEAVES, PLUS A FEW TORN ONES

1 RED ONION, PEELED

250 G (9 OZ) MUSHROOMS, SUCH AS SWISS BROWN, FIELD...

1 CARROT, PEELED

200 G (7 OZ) ZUCCHINI (COURGETTES)

3 LARGE TOMATOES

1 GREEK COFFEE CUP (ABOUT 4 TABLESPOONS) OLIVE OIL

100 G (3½ OZ/½ CUP) MEDIUM-GRAIN RICE

3 TABLESPOONS CHOPPED FLAT-LEAF PARSLEY

½ TABLESPOON DRIED MINT

JUICE OF 1 LEMON

3 TABLESPOONS GRATED KEFALOTIRI OR PARMESAN CHEESE

This wonderful way comes from my friend Artemis' mum, Christina. It is a more unusual vegetarian version than you may find readily available in Greece and completely delicious.

It is very easy to double the quantity, and they keep well for the next day, so it's worth making a good amount. Christina makes at least 70 at a time – it can be fun to sit at a table and work, hopefully with someone helping you.

If using bought leaves, put them in a bowl of water to soak for a few minutes. Drain, pat dry with paper towels then stack in piles for later. Using the large holes of a grater, grate the onion, mushrooms, carrot, zucchini and tomato, keeping them separate for now. Heat 3 tablespoons of oil in a wide pot and sauté the onion until golden. Add the mushrooms, carrot, zucchini and rice and sauté for 10 minutes or so. Add the grated tomato, parsley, mint and lemon juice and season with salt and black pepper. Simmer for 5 minutes. Remove from the heat and stir in the kefalotiri.

Preheat the oven to 180°c (350°f/gas 4). Spread a few whole vine leaves at a time on your work surface, shiny side down. Spoon a heaped tablespoon of filling onto each leaf and roll up neatly and snugly, tucking in the sides after the first roll and continuing to roll. Line them up in the dish. They should just fit but if not, stack the last few on top. Grate the remaining tomato (so that the skin stays behind in your hand) and scatter it over the top of the dolmades. Add 250 ml (9 fl oz/ 1 cup) of water and drizzle over the remaining oil. Sprinkle with salt and pepper. Rock the dish 2 or 3 times to distribute the liquid. Cover with foil. Bake for 1 hour, uncover and bake for 10 minutes or so.

HALVA TIS NIKOKIRAS HOUSEWIVES' HALVA

Χαλβάς

SERVES AN EXTENDED FAMILY

250 ML (9 FL OZ/1 CUP) OLIVE OIL

100 G (3½ OZ/²/₃ CUP) ALMONDS, WITH SKIN ON, COARSELY CHOPPED

200 G (7 OZ/1 CUP) FINE SEMOLINA

200 G (7 OZ/1 CUP) COARSE SEMOLINA

GROUND CINNAMON, TO SERVE

SYRUP

500 G (1 LB 2 OZ) SUGAR

JUICE OF ½ LEMON

LONG STRIP OF LEMON RIND

1 CINNAMON ROLL

3 WHOLE CLOVES

This is great for fasting purposes before Easter. At other times butter can be used instead of the oil if you like. It's a rather unusual cake and Greeks appreciate it for what it is. I have received many puzzled expressions when serving it to non-Greeks. Housewives have a code for this recipe: 1 2 3 4. The 1 is for the cup of oil, 2 for the semolina, 3 for the sugar and 4 for the water. I have strayed slightly from the code here in terms of the sugar, which I use a little less of. You could also add a couple of tablespoons of rose or orange blossom water to the syrup once it's finished simmering.

For the syrup, put the sugar, lemon juice and rind, cinnamon roll and cloves into a pot with 1 litre (35 fl oz/4 cups) of water and bring to the boil. Simmer for 10 minutes or so.

Warm the oil in a big heavy-based pot. Add the almonds and cook over medium heat, stirring, until lightly toasted. Stir in the semolinas and dry roast them too until a bit golden here and there, stirring constantly and taking care that it doesn't burn.

Lightly oil a 1.5 litre (52 fl oz /6 cup) capacity savarin or ring tin with a little oil on a paper towel. Scoop out the lemon rind and spices from the syrup then gradually stir the syrup into the roasting semolina. Take care when you pour it in as it will bubble and splash. Stir constantly over low heat until the liquid is all absorbed by the semolina and it comes away from the side of the pot. Remove from the heat and scrape out into the tin. Flatten with the back of a soup spoon or spatula to push out any creases or small spaces. Let it cool for a few minutes, then ease the halva away from the sides of the tin in a few places using a thin knife. Quickly turn the tin over and unmould the halva onto a flat plate. Scatter with the ground cinnamon and cut into slivers to serve. You only need thin pieces.

Alternatively there is the beautiful marble-looking slab of halva, available in Greek food stores and delicatessens, which is called 'the grocers' halva' (halva tou mpakali). Some are plain others have nuts and some are in swirls alternating chocolate and plain halva. It is made of tahini and is very rich and nutritious and just small slivers can be carved off as a snack. As a dessert, the plain version is wonderful in a chunk or small slice served with a scattering of cinnamon over and a squeeze of lemon. This is eaten throughout the year but more so during fasting times.

The 25th of March, Independence Day, is a national holiday commemorating the first day in 1821 of the liberation struggle against the Ottomans. It is also Annunciation Day so is a double celebration. As it is in the Easter fasting period, the traditional dish for the day is fried salt cod with skordalia.

SKORDALIA GARLIC POTATO + OLIVE OIL MASH

Σκορδαλιά

MAKES A NICE BOWLFUL

600 G (1 LB 5 OZ) UNPEELED POTATOES, WASHED

8 GARLIC CLOVES, PEELED

JUICE OF 2 LEMONS

ABOUT 185 ML (6 FL OZ/ ¾ CUP) OLIVE OIL

You have got to have nice fresh garlic here. Not old tired cloves, but ones that give you an apple-type crunch when you start chopping. I have also seen things like the garlic being roasted or blanched in some lemon juice to get rid of some of its knock-down properties, but it's not really the real thing. And although you might feel awful breath-wise after this, it's well worth it. (Plus haven't they always said that garlic gets rid of mosquitoes and is great against colds and flu? So just see this as preventative medicine, really you are just doing yourself ounces of good.)

Skordalia goes very well with other fried foods such as keftedes. If you are poaching some fish and happen to have some fish broth, then stir in a few tablespoons of that instead of the water to thin it out and add flavour. 'And this,' says Kiria Fotini from the Stavros museum in Ithaka, the inflections in her voice showing her love for the island as she rattled away her skordalia tricks. 'This', she emphasised again, slapping her hand down onto the table, 'is the whole secret. The trick that many people don't know. It takes it to a different level entirely,' she finished, then indicating a goblet from which Odysseus may have drunk.

If you like, you can even make a bowl of some extra cloves of garlic crushed to a pulp and covered with olive oil, to serve to those who really want a tremendous amount as some might find the 8 garlic cloves in here a bit conservative. This keeps well in the fridge, covered, for 5 to 6 days.

The strength of the garlic mellows over this time.

Boil the potatoes in their skins in salted water until soft. While they are cooking, smash the garlic cloves with a little salt to a purée using a mortar and pestle. When the potatoes are just cool enough to handle, peel off their skins and pass the potatoes through a ricer into a tall bowl. Add the puréed garlic and pour in the lemon juice and olive oil. Beat in briskly with a wooden spoon until amalgamated and smooth. Season well with salt and pepper to taste; it needs a good amount of salt to bring out the flavours. Stir in 3 tablespoons or so of hot water or better still, hot fish broth if you have any. Serve with the fried salt cod.

BAKALIAROS SKORDALIA FRIED SALT COD

Μπακαλιάρος σκορδαλιά

SERVES 4

4 PIECES (ABOUT 180 G/
6½ OZ EACH) BONELESS
SALT COD FILLET, SKIN ON

PLAIN (ALL-PURPOSE)
FLOUR, FOR COATING

LIGHT OLIVE OIL,
FOR FRYING

LEMON QUARTERS,
FOR SERVING

SKORDALIA (PAGE 66),
FOR SERVING

You could also use other fresh white fish fillets here which would of course have no need for soaking. (Remember to sprinkle some salt on those when serving, though.)

The salt cod will need soaking for 2 to 3 days – and even then you should taste a small piece to see that it's not too salty before frying (the thinner tail end will be the saltiest part). It is also possible to get ready soaked cod in some places.

People make this at home on the 25th of March but many also go out to a restaurant. I ate it in a restaurant that served only these things: fried salt cod with skordalia, a plate of black-eyed beans, fava and a dish of olives, and then there was only halva for dessert. There was nothing else on the menu. Wine came from a barrel downstairs – what a restaurant!

To prepare the salt cod, put it in a bowl and cover with plenty of cold water. Cover the bowl with plastic wrap and refrigerate for 2 to 3 days, changing the water twice a day. You can taste a tiny piece to check that it's not too salty. If it is, you need to soak it for longer in fresh water. Rinse the fillets and dry well with paper towels. Put the flour in a deep plate, and fill a deep bowl with cold water.

Add enough olive oil to a large frying pan to come halfway up the sides of the fish. Heat the oil. Pat the fillets in the flour, coating both sides. Quickly dip them in the cold water, let the excess drip off, then pat in the flour again. Fry, skin side down, and when that is crisp, golden and firm, turn them over and do the other side. Drain on paper towels. Serve with a grinding of pepper and lemon quarters and a good dollop of skordalia on the side.

AMSTEL
MYTHOS
WINE
OUZO
FANTA O
FANTA L
ICE TEA
ICE TEA
COCA C
COLA LI
SPRITE
SODA
WATER
GREEK COF
ICE COFFEE
NES COFFE

FASTING

FOODS

There is grand security I find, in Greece, in the presence of priests – and being physically near them. I love to be, for example, travelling with a priest or two on a boat. And if by chance the boat about to leave was suddenly cancelled, I would definitely say it was for the better.

FAVA PURÉED SPLIT YELLOW PEAS

Φάβα

MAKES 4 CUPS

500 G (1 LB 2 OZ) FAVA

1 SMALL RED ONION, PEELED

2 GARLIC CLOVES, PEELED

ABOUT 1½ TEASPOONS SALT

OLIVE OIL, FOR SERVING

1 LARGE RED ONION, SLICED, FOR SERVING

HANDFUL OF CAPERS WITH LEAVES, FOR SERVING

Fava are dried, split yellow peas that, when boiled, melt into a creamy purée. This is great splashed with olive oil, pepper, capers and chunks of sweet red onions. It can be served as a meze with bread and cheese. It also works beautifully next to a main course, for example with the grilled lamb chops. It is very easy to make, you could really just follow the instructions on the packet you buy. If you have made it beforehand, you will need to add some water and heat it to thin out again to a soft, creamy mash, as it will have set in a clump.

Rinse the fava, then put into a pot and cover with cold water. Bring to the boil. Drain and give the fava a shower in a colander. Rinse out the pot, put the fava back in and add 1 litre (35 fl oz/4 cups) hot water. Bring to the boil, add the whole onion and garlic and simmer, partly covered, for about 30 minutes. Remove the lid and simmer over low heat, stirring from time to time, for about 30 minutes more or until all the water has been absorbed and it starts glooping on the surface. Stir in the salt to taste. Discard the onion and garlic cloves and pulse the fava, with a hand-held blender if you have one, or in a food processor until smooth like soft mashed potato – much will have collapsed on its own and it may not even be necessary to purée. Leave it to sit for a bit then spoon into a serving dish. Drizzle a good amount of olive oil over the top. Serve warm with the onion slices, capers and a grinding of pepper.

MAVROMATIKA BLACK-EYED BEANS (AND LENTILS)

Μαυρομάτικα (με φακές)

SERVES 8 OR SO

250 G (9 OZ/1¼ CUPS) BLACK-EYED BEANS

1 SMALL RED ONION, PEELED

2 GARLIC CLOVES, PEELED

100 G (3½ OZ) BROWN LENTILS, RINSED AND DRAINED

6 TABLESPOONS OLIVE OIL, PLUS EXTRA FOR SERVING

3 TABLESPOONS RED WINE VINEGAR

40 G (1½ OZ) ROUND SPRING ONIONS, CHOPPED

4 HEAPED TABLESPOONS ROUGHLY CHOPPED FLAT-LEAF PARSLEY

2 TABLESPOONS ROUGHLY CHOPPED DILL

Often, plain boiled black-eyed beans are served crowded onto a small plate with a pile of chopped onions and parsley and a splashing of olive oil. This is just an all-mixed-in-together version with a couple of extra accessories.

It is wonderful served with a dish of feta, a dish of olives, a small dish of chopped tomatoes and some bread. Tuna works very well on the side too.

Soak the beans in plenty of cold water overnight. Next day drain and rinse them, then put into a pot and cover well with cold water. Bring to the boil. Drain and rinse out the pot. Give the beans a shower in a colander then return to the pot with fresh water. Add the red onion and garlic cloves and bring to the boil, skimming the surface when necessary. Lower the heat and simmer for about 30 minutes. Add the lentils and simmer for another 30 minutes or so, until tender but not mushy. Add some salt in the last 5 or 10 minutes.

When done, drain the beans and lentils well through a fine sieve. Discard the onion and whole garlic cloves if you can find them. Put into a bowl to cool a bit.

Add the oil, vinegar, spring onion, parsley and dill to the bowl and season with extra salt, if necessary, and a few grinds of pepper. Turn through very gently. Serve warm or at room temperature, with an extra drizzle of olive oil over individual servings.

TAHINOSOUPA TAHINI SOUP

Ταχινόσουπα

SERVES 4

2 TEASPOONS SESAME
SEEDS

½ TEASPOON PAPRIKA

SPRINKLING OF GROUND
CHILLI, OPTIONAL

1 TEASPOON GRATED
LEMON ZEST

ABOUT 150 G (5½ OZ)
FRESH EGG-FREE NOODLES
(HILOPITES, PAGE 81), OR
80 G (2¾ OZ) DRIED

130 G (4¾ OZ/½ CUP) TAHINI

JUICE OF 1½ LEMONS

OLIVE OIL, FOR SERVING

This is a very simple soup that can be made in minutes. Traditionally it's from the Cycladic Islands and is eaten in the week leading up to Easter, or on Good Friday when simple meat-free foods are eaten.

Toast the sesame seeds lightly in a small dry frying pan. Add the paprika and the chilli, if using, and cook briefly, taking care not to burn it. Stir the lemon zest through and remove from the pan to a small bowl.

Bring 1 litre (35 fl oz/4 cups) of water to the boil in a pot with some salt. Add the hilopites and boil until just tender, about 2 minutes, or according to the packet instructions if dried.

Meanwhile, put the tahini and lemon juice into a bowl, add a ladleful of the boiling hilopites water and whisk until smooth. When the hilopites are ready, pour the tahini mixture in and stir gently over the heat for a couple of minutes. Taste for salt. Serve in bowls with a dribble of olive oil, a scattering of the sesame paprika mixture and a grind of pepper.

HILOPITES NOODLES

Χυλοπίτες

MAKES ABOUT 150 G (5½ OZ)

100 G (3½ OZ/²⁄₃ CUP) PLAIN
(ALL-PURPOSE) FLOUR
3 TEASPOONS OLIVE OIL

Hilopites are Greek-style noodles/pasta that are served on the side of some dishes or in soups. They are available dried, in packets, from Greek grocers or you can make your own. These egg-free hilopites are good for the fasting period.

Stir the flour with a pinch of salt into a bowl. Add the olive oil and about 1½ tablespoons of water and mix into a loose dough with a wooden spoon. Now bring it together with your hands and knead for 1 to 2 minutes, adding a little more flour if necessary to give a smooth, quite dry dough. Rest at room temperature, covered loosely with a tea towel, for 30 minutes or so. Roll out very thinly, until almost see-through, on a dry surface that has been only very lightly floured. Cut into strips of about 2 cm (¾ inch), then cut those up into rough rectangles of 3 to 4 cm (1¼ to 1½ inch). The hilopites can be left out to dry a little for easier handling (they will be less likely to stick together) for 30 minutes or so, but it's not necessary. If you try to completely dry long strands, they will tend to break into smaller lengths, but for the tahinosoupa it is not a problem.

SOUPIES ME HORTA
SQUID WITH GREENS

Σουπιές με χόρτα

SERVES 4

850 G (1 LB 14 OZ) SMALL–MEDIUM SQUID

400 G (14 OZ) TRIMMED GREENS, CHOPPED INTO BIG PIECES

4 TABLESPOONS OLIVE OIL

3 GARLIC CLOVES, CHOPPED

GOOD PINCH OF GROUND RED CHILLI

200 G (7 OZ) TIN DICED TOMATOES

125 ML (4½ FL OZ/½ CUP) WHITE WINE

This is good made with spinach, silverbeet (swiss chard), chicory (witlof), mustard greens, or a couple of these in combination. It is healthy, and really a dish based just on its ingredients – what you put in is exactly what you will get in flavour. The chunks of greens work well with the chunks of squid. You could use calamari – it wouldn't need as long to cook, and would be more delicate.

Cut the heads off and pull the innards from the squid. Pull the quill out of the body. Cut off the tentacles just above the eyes. Rinse the bodies and tentacles in cold water and dry them on paper towels. Slice the bodies open, lay them flat and cut into large slices or chunks.

Rinse the greens and keep in a colander. Heat the oil and garlic in a non-stick frying pan until you can smell the garlic. Add the squid and sauté on a high heat for a few minutes. Add the chilli and tomato, cook for a few minutes to soften, then add some salt and pepper and the wine. When much of the wine has evaporated add 125 ml (4 fl oz/ ½ cup) of water. Cover, lower the heat and simmer for 15 to 20 minutes or until the squid is tender when you poke a piece with a fork.

Add the greens to the squid with about 250 ml (9 fl oz/1 cup) of water and bring back to bubbling. Season with a little salt, cover, and simmer for 12 to 15 minutes – the greens should be softened and there should be a nice amount of reduced sauce to hold the dish together.

HTAPODI ME KOFTO MAKARONAKI OCTOPUS WITH SHORT PASTA

Χταπόδι με κοφτό μακαρονάκι

SERVES 4 TO 6

1 MEDIUM OCTOPUS (ABOUT 800 G/1 LB 12 OZ)

5 TABLESPOONS OLIVE OIL

1 RED ONION, CHOPPED

½ TEASPOON PAPRIKA

2 GARLIC CLOVES, CHOPPED

1 BAY LEAF

PINCH OF GROUND CHILLI

125 ML (4½ FL OZ/½ CUP) RED WINE

400 G (14 OZ) TIN CRUSHED TOMATOES

2 TABLESPOONS CHOPPED FLAT-LEAF PARSLEY

250 G (9 OZ) DITALINI

2 TABLESPOONS COARSELY CHOPPED FLAT-LEAF PARSLEY, EXTRA TO SERVE

Here the octopus is baked and then the just-boiled pasta is mixed through to produce a single tasty dish. You can also use a small rice-shaped pasta such as risoni or orzo, or even just a heap of spaghetti on the side is lovely.

To prepare the octopus, cut the tentacles off just below the eyes. Push the beak out from the centre of the tentacles and cut the hard eyes from the head. Cut the head up one side being careful to avoid the ink sac, and scrape out the innards. Rinse under cold running water and pat dry with paper towels. Cut the tentacles diagonally into 4 to 5 cm (1½ to 2 inch) lengths, and slice the body into similar-sized pieces.

Preheat the oven to 180°c (350°f/gas 4). Heat the oil in a large frying pan and sauté the onion until softened. Add the octopus, paprika, garlic, bay leaf and chilli and cook until the octopus brightens in colour and turns purpley. Add the wine, bring to the boil, reduce heat to low and simmer for 10 minutes or so. Add the tomato, parsley, and salt and pepper and bring back to bubbling point. Scrape out into a roasting dish of about 22 x 30 cm (8½ x 12 inches). Bake in the oven for 45 minutes or so, checking once or twice that there is enough liquid. If needed, add a little hot water to keep the sauce thick but loose.

Meanwhile, cook the pasta in boiling salted water until tender. Drain. Add to the octopus dish and mix through. Serve scattered with the extra parsley and black pepper.

SPANAKORIZO SPINACH RICE

Σπανακόριζο

SERVES 4

1 KG (2 LB 4 OZ) SPINACH, RINSED, DRAINED

4 TABLESPOONS OLIVE OIL

100 G (3½ OZ) ROUND SPRING ONIONS WITH SOME GREEN, CHOPPED

3 TABLESPOONS CHOPPED DILL

200 G (7 OZ) MEDIUM-GRAIN RICE

JUICE OF 1 SMALL LEMON

1 TABLESPOON CHOPPED FRESH MINT

I love putting such amounts of green stuff into a pot. Makes me feel like I am on the right track. You will need a big wide pot here. Choose lovely small spinach where you hardly have to discard any tough stalks. I have added some mint here to the traditional recipe. I love this with lots of lemon squeezed over, and pepper, and with a good dollop of Yoghurt on the side (page 131, made without any of the spices).

Roughly chop the spinach leaves. Heat the olive oil in a very large pot and sauté the onions until pale gold and softened. Add the dill and sauté for 30 seconds or so then stir in the rice.

Now add the spinach. You might feel that it won't all fit in the pot, but squash in as much as you can. Add 500 ml (17 fl oz/2 cups) of hot water and squash and turn the spinach until it begins to wilt and it's all in. Add a good amount of salt, turn the spinach over with a wooden spoon and put the lid on. Bring to the boil then turn through again. Lower the heat and simmer, covered, for about 15 minutes. If there is still water in the bottom of the pot towards the end of this time, take the lid off and turn up the heat to let it evaporate. Remove from the heat. Sprinkle in the lemon juice and add a good few grinds of pepper. Turn through gently and taste for salt. Add the mint. Cover with a clean tea towel, put the lid back on and leave for 10 minutes to steam. Serve hot or even at room temperature.

MIDOPILAFO MUSSEL RICE

Μυδοπίλαφο

SERVES 4 TO 6

1.5 KG (3 LB 5 OZ) BLACK MUSSELS, NOT TOO BIG

6 TABLESPOONS OLIVE OIL

3 GARLIC CLOVES, 1 WHOLE, 2 CHOPPED

2 THICK FLAT-LEAF PARSLEY STALKS WITH LEAVES

125 ML (4 FL OZ/½ CUP) WHITE WINE

180 G (6½ OZ) ROUND SPRING ONIONS, CHOPPED WITH SOME GREEN ALSO

4 TABLESPOONS COARSELY CHOPPED DILL, PLUS EXTRA, CHOPPED, FOR SERVING

3 TABLESPOONS OUZO

2 TOMATOES, GRATED ON THE LARGE HOLES OF A GRATER (SO THAT THE SKIN STAYS BEHIND IN YOUR HAND)

400 G (14 OZ) MEDIUM-GRAIN RICE

This is often made with all the shells removed, so if you prefer you can make it that way too (I love the shells). This is a dish from northern Greece, which is best served warm just after you have made it. It is great alone, or along with other fish plates as part of a meze. Choose lovely fresh mussels. Nice with ouzo on ice.

De-beard the mussels and scrub them clean with a wire brush under running water. Drain. Give each one a tap and discard those which stay open. Heat 2 tablespoons of the oil in a high-sided pot large enough to hold all the mussels. Add the whole garlic and when it starts to smell good, add the drained mussels, parsley and wine. Put over high heat and cook, covered, until the mussels have opened. Remove the opened ones and give the others another chance. Remove from the heat and strain, keeping the liquid. Now discard any mussels that have not opened. When cool enough to handle remove half of the mussels from their shells. Discard the empty shells and put the mussels together with the other ones still in their shells. Keep aside for now.

Heat the rest of the oil in a wide non-stick pot. Add the onion and sauté on a low heat until soft and golden. Stir in the chopped garlic and half the dill and when they smell good, add the ouzo. Cook until it evaporates, then add the tomato. Increase the heat to medium and simmer for a few minutes, then add the rice, turning it through to coat well. Make the mussel broth up to 1 litre (35 fl oz/4 cups) with hot water and add this to the pot with a little salt. Bring to the boil, lower the heat and simmer for about 10 to 12 minutes or until a lot of the liquid has been absorbed. Taste, adding salt if necessary. Add all the mussels,

continued

*shelled and unshelled, turn through
with a wooden spoon and simmer
for another 5 minutes, checking that
nothing sticks to the bottom of the
pot. Remove from the heat, add the
remaining dill and fluff up the rice.
Cover the pot with a clean tea towel.
Put the lid back on and leave it for
another 10 minutes or so to steam
and finish cooking.*

*Serve with a grind of pepper
and a scattering of the extra dill.*

Many people will have been fasting up to the point of Easter Saturday. Many for as long as 40 days. First thing then on the Saturday morning, they will go (with nil by mouth) to take communion, then at 11.30 pm they will set off for the lithurgy at church with their shiny shoes and their good clothes. Everyone has brought a lambada (a candle of natural wax) which must be lit from the holy light which works like this: every year a new light is lit in Jerusalem. The story goes that the patriarchis (head of the Orthodox church) goes down into the grave of Jesus holding a bunch of candles and by miraculous action the candles get lit. Up he comes with the candles to the representatives of all churches, and each one lights up and takes their candles back to their respective countries. The Greek one travels back by charter and upon arrival in Athens a small fleet of helicopters and cars whizz off in various directions with their lighted candles. Priests can be seen then landing in helicopters outside major cathedrals to light the main candle before jetting off once more to light up other towns. Provincial priests are waiting at the cathedrals to light up and move on to their smaller churches, and so it goes until eventually the entire nation's candles are ablaze. This symbolically is the fotissi (enlightenment) of the people. When the priests in the churches give the light to all the people, everything starts to light up in a slow and steady ripple, until a whole country is shining. Then you know that the Greeks have got something special, because they have this faith – and I love them for their details. With their lit candles they go home well after midnight, many drawing a black cross with their candle flame under their doorframe to bless the house before entering. Then they crack their red eggs and whip the egg and lemon sauce into the lamb's intestine soup before eating it, and call it a day. (A foreigner alighting upon this scene slightly earlier may be surprised to find all tables set and not a soul in sight.) Next day comes the lamb on the spit, which can be seen turning in many corners of the country, and there will be many others roasting and grilling in different kitchens.

MAYIRITSA EASTER SOUP

Μαγειρίτσα

SERVES ABOUT 8

1 LAMB SIKOTARIA OR 'PLUCK' (ABOUT 1.2 KG/ 2 LB 10 OZ)

500 G (1 LB 2 OZ) LAMB INTESTINES

COARSE SALT, FOR RUBBING

1 LEMON, FOR CLEANING

2 TABLESPOONS BUTTER (ABOUT 40 G/1½ OZ)

80 G (2¾ OZ) TRIMMED ROUND SPRING ONIONS, CHOPPED

200 G (7 OZ/1 CUP) MEDIUM-GRAIN RICE

1 LARGE HANDFUL CHOPPED DILL

7 MINT LEAVES

2 EGG YOLKS

JUICE OF 3 LEMONS

This lamb intestine and sikotaria soup is traditionally made and eaten after the Easter midnight mass. This is the recipe of Manos' mum, Aleka, which the family always makes. This is mostly prepared beforehand, then when everyone comes home from midnight Mass, the egg and lemon sauce is whipped up as the last-minute preparation. A vegetarian mayiritsa is sometimes made using mushrooms.

Put the pluck in a large pot, cover with water and bring to the boil. Simmer for 20 minutes, skimming the surface of scum. Strain, reserving the broth. You will need about 1 litre (35 fl oz/4 cups) for the soup. Cut the pluck into small irregular pieces.

Turn the intestines inside out with a skewer, rub with coarse salt and lemon to clean, then rinse and drain. If you don't turn them inside out, then cut into pieces. Cut the intestines into pieces of a similar size to the pluck. Rub between your hands with salt and lemon, then put in a bowl. Cover with water and leave for 10 minutes. Drain, rinse, then blanch in boiling water for 5 minutes. Rinse and drain.

Heat the butter in a large heavy-based pot and sauté the onion until softened. Add the pluck and intestines. Fry for a minute or 2, stirring, then add the reserved broth, 500 ml (17 fl oz/2 cups) of water and bring to the boil. Add the rice, and season well with salt and pepper. Simmer, uncovered, on low heat for about 20 minutes or until the meats are tender. Add the dill and mint and let it sit for a few minutes before serving. Remove the pot from the heat. Whisk the yolks and lemon juice in a bowl. Stir a little of the hot broth in to acclimatise it, then slowly stir the lot back into the pot. Serve immediately.

TSOUREKI PLAITED EASTER BREAD

Τσουρέκι

SERVES A FAMILY & FRIENDS

30 G (1 OZ) FRESH YEAST, OR 1 TABLESPOON (14 G/ ½ OZ) DRIED

120 G (4¼ OZ) SUGAR, PLUS EXTRA, FOR DUSTING

185 ML (6 FL OZ/¾ CUP) LUKEWARM MILK

630 G (1 LB 6 OZ) PLAIN (ALL-PURPOSE) FLOUR

½ TEASPOON MASTICHA GRANULES

½ TEASPOON FRESHLY GRATED NUTMEG

2 TEASPOONS ANISE SEEDS, TOASTED, GROUND

¼ TEASPOON SALT

120 G (4¼ OZ) UNSALTED BUTTER, MELTED

2 EGGS, LIGHTLY WHISKED, PLUS 1 EXTRA, WHISKED, FOR BRUSHING

2 TABLESPOONS BRANDY

1 RED EGG (PAGE 104), OPTIONAL

A red egg is set into the top of the plait before baking. Different spices are often used in this bread and flaked almonds are sometimes scattered on top before baking. Many people like it just plain. Here there is masticha (ground resin from the masticha tree). You can leave it out for a plainer taste if you prefer. If possible, get the whole anise seeds here and grind them yourself for the lovely smell. Tsoureki is enjoyed for breakfast also and is lovely toasted and buttered.

Crumble or scatter the yeast into a wide basin. Sneak a teaspoon of sugar from your amount and add to the yeast, and pour in the milk. Whisk in 3 handfuls of the flour to give a smooth batter. Cover with a tea towel and leave for half an hour or so in a warm place to activate and bubble up.

Grind the masticha with a teaspoon or so of the sugar to a powder. Mix the nutmeg, anise, masticha, sugar and salt through the remaining flour and add to the batter. Add the butter, 2 eggs and brandy. Mix it first with a wooden spoon then change to your hands when a loose dough forms. Remove your rings (remember where you have put them!) and start kneading. Knead for 6 to 7 minutes, until you have a lovely smooth and spongy dough. Add more flour if necessary to give a firm dough. Wipe out the bowl with an oiled paper towel. Put the dough in, cover with plastic wrap then the tea towel, and put another cloth on as well. Put in a warm place for about 2 hours until it has puffed up to double its size.

Punch the dough down and knead it a couple of times. Separate it into 3 equal portions, weighing them if necessary. Gently stretch, tease and roll each into long ropes of about 36 cm (14¼ inches). Line them up side by side on your work surface and press three ends together. Now plait them tightly and evenly, finishing with the tail ends pressed together and twisted underneath. Put onto a baking tray, which has been lined with baking paper,

pressing in the two ends of the plait like you're playing an accordion to give a loaf of about 28 cm (11¼ inch) long. Cover loosely with a tea towel and return to the warm spot until risen again, about 1 hour.

Preheat the oven to 180°c (350°f/gas 4). Brush the top of the loaf with the extra egg and scatter the extra sugar over. Now nestle the red egg into the folds of the bread at one end. Bake until golden and sounds hollow when tapped, 25 to 30 minutes. Cool on a wire rack before serving.

PASKALINA AVGA RED EGGS

Πασχαλινά (Κόκκινα) αυγά

MAKES 12 RED EGGS

12 EGGS

1 SACHET (½ TEASPOON)
GREEK RED POWDERED
EGG DYE, CHEMICAL-FREE
IF POSSIBLE

125 ML (4 FL OZ/½ CUP)
WHITE WINE VINEGAR

OLIVE OIL, FOR POLISHING

Part of the Easter preparations is the dyeing of eggs. Mainly red, to represent the blood of Christ, but sometimes people use other colours. The eggs are polished with a drop of olive oil to make them lovely and shiny. These are sitting pretty in their baskets, just waiting to be cracked. The tradition is that you have to crack eggs after church and on Easter Sunday, and you must crack tops to tops, and bottoms to bottoms with another contestant. The strongest egg wins. Over the next day or so they are peeled and cut into wedges and splashed with vinegar, olive oil, salt, pepper and paprika. One or more unpeeled ones will have been set into the tsoureki to bake. Even if they are over-boiled and greying and bleeding dye, everyone loves the eggs and eats them after cracking.

Lower the eggs gently into a pot where they will fit close together in a single layer. Cover with water (room temperature). Bring slowly to the boil so that they don't bounce and crack. Simmer for a few minutes then turn off the heat and leave them in the water for 10 minutes or so to cool and finish cooking. Drain.

Dissolve the dye in a cup of hot water. Put 500 ml (17 fl oz/2 cups) of water (room temperature) and the vinegar in a bowl large enough to take 6 eggs with room between them. Stir in the dye and lower half the eggs in. If needed, add enough water to cover the eggs making sure no tips or tops are sticking out. Leave for 2 to 3 minutes, rolling them around with a spoon once or twice so that the same part of them isn't always touching the bottom of the dish. Scoop out with a slotted spoon and drain on a plate lined with paper towels. Repeat with the remaining eggs.

As they are drying, roll the eggs over on the paper towels so that the undersides dry too. When they are all dry, polish with a paper towel dipped in olive oil. The dye will wash off plates and bowls, but might need a little scrubbing if you get some on your hands, so use gloves if you prefer.

I PALIA I KOTA EHI TO ZOUMI – THE OLD HEN HAS THE BROTH

ARNI LEMONATO LEMON + OREGANO LAMB

Αρνί λεμονάτο

SERVES 4 TO 6

375 ML (13 FL OZ/1½ CUPS)
FRESH LEMON JUICE
(6 TO 7 LEMONS)

125 ML (4 OZ/½ CUP)
OLIVE OIL

1 HEAPED TABLESPOON
DRIED OREGANO

1.5 KG (3 LB 5 OZ) LEG OF
LAMB, BONE HACKED IN
ONE PLACE AND HINGED,
SO IT FITS IN THE DISH

1.2 KG (2 LB 10 OZ)
POTATOES, CUT INTO
NICE BIG CHUNKS

This is sooooo lemony. It is also a dish that you can really leave in the oven and go out shopping for a while and hardly even think about the fact that you left something in the oven.

This recipe is my friend Marion's way. She says to keep turning the lamb while it's marinating and spooning some of the marinade over every waking hour or so – she did say not to worry about it while sleeping. I use a large round (about 33 cm/13 inches in diameter) or rectangular dish here. You may have to ask your butcher to hack once into the leg (so it fits in the dish).

Mix the lemon juice, olive oil and oregano with 375 ml (13 fl oz /1½ cups) of water in a large non-corrosive baking dish. Rub the lamb well all over with salt and black pepper and put it in the marinade. Turn it over a couple of times to coat well. Cover with plastic wrap and refrigerate for 24 hours, turning it frequently throughout your waking hours.

Preheat the oven to 180°c (350°f/gas 4). Cover the lamb with a sheet of baking paper and then cover the dish tightly with 3 layers of foil. Bake for 1 hour. Turn the lamb over, cover again and reduce the heat to 150°c (300°f/gas 2). Bake the lamb for another 2 hours. Now turn the lamb gently as it will be very tender. Add the potatoes to the dish and sprinkle a little salt over them. Cover again and bake for 2 hours, turning the potatoes once during this time. Remove the foil, shuffle the potatoes and put back in the oven at 200°c (400°f/gas 6). Roast until a little golden here and there, 20 to 30 minutes. Remove from the oven and rest the lamb for 5 minutes before serving.

GALAKTOBOUREKO CUSTARD PHYLLO PIE

Γαλακτομπούρεκο

SERVES 12

120 G (4¼ OZ) UNSALTED
BUTTER, MELTED TO
GOLDEN

12 SHEETS PHYLLO*, AT
LEAST 30 X 38 CM (12 X
15 INCHES) IN SIZE

SYRUP

280 G (10 OZ) SUGAR

1 LONG STRIP OF
LEMON PEEL

FILLING

225 G (8 Z) SUGAR

75 G (2½ OZ) FINE
SEMOLINA

20 G (¾ OZ) CORNFLOUR

4 EGG YOLKS, PLUS
2 WHOLE EGGS

1.5 LITRES (52 FL OZ/
6 CUPS) MILK

2 TEASPOONS VANILLA
EXTRACT

A NICE GRATING OF
FRESH NUTMEG

This is my friend Annette's recipe. She is very good with desserts. I love the pureness of this pie. Syrupy Greek sweets are always served with a glass of cold water. Greeks have always loved making an outing to a café or zaharoplasteio (confectioners) to have a sweet. This is often the type of sweet you will find served after Easter lamb.

Butter should be heated and melted to a nice golden caramelly colour for good flavour, and while you are making this, you will probably have to put the butter back onto the stove to melt again when it hardens a bit.

To make the syrup, put the sugar and lemon peel in a small saucepan and add 185 ml (6 fl oz/¾ cup) of water. Put over a medium heat and stir until the sugar dissolves. Bring to the boil and simmer for about 5 minutes. Remove from the heat and cool. Preheat the oven to 175°c (325°f/gas 3).

For the filling put the sugar, semolina and cornflour in the bowl of an electric mixer. Add all the eggs and beat until thick and pale. Heat the milk, vanilla and nutmeg in a large saucepan to just below boiling. Add a ladleful to the eggs and mix in. Add another ladleful, mix, and continue until all the milk has been added. Scrape back into the pot and return it to the heat on low for 5 or 10 minutes, whisking often until it is very thick and nothing sticks to the bottom. When it's thickened and glooping and is just at the point before boiling, remove from the heat.

Have the phyllo sheets ready, covered by a tea towel to prevent them drying out. Brush the base and sides of a 22 x 30 cm (8½ x 12 inch) ovenproof dish with butter.

Lay 1 sheet of phyllo on your work surface and brush with butter. Cover with another sheet, brush it with butter and continue in this way until you have a stack of 6 sheets. Lift them up and fit into the buttered dish, covering the base and sides. Press them gently into the corners of the dish to make a nest for the filling. Pour the filling on top and smooth the surface.

Make another stack of 6 buttered phyllo sheets. Lift this onto the pie, covering the filling. Press the two overhanging layers of phyllo together, trimming these to a couple of centimetres (about an inch). Roll these edges over on themselves to seal the filling in. Using a sharp knife, gently score the top pastry into 12 pieces , only cutting through the top sheet or two of phyllo. Flick a little cold water here and there (to prevent the phyllo curling). Bake until crisp and golden, about 25 minutes. Remove from the oven, rest for a couple of minutes then pour the syrup over the top, covering all the pie. Now leave for at least 1 hour before serving to allow the syrup to settle as the pie cools.

Will keep for a number of days if left, covered wth a tea towel, in a cool dry place (not refrigerated).

✿ The phyllo sheets need to be large enough to cover the base and sides of a 22 x 30 cm (8½ x 12 inch) dish. If yours are smaller, use more sheets and cut to fit.

MEZEDES

SHARED FOODS

The Greeks seem to have inherited such a natural sense of community. An ease of hospitality through which young and old move so easily. They can attach on new and sudden situations or people so smoothly – as though all of life were just one long Greek dance. And grandparents, babies and friends and relatives of every generation are sharing plates of starters on long tables.

SAGANAKI FRIED CHEESE

Σαγανάκι

SERVES 4

LIGHT OLIVE OIL,
FOR FRYING

1 EGG, LIGHTLY BEATEN

PLAIN (ALL-PURPOSE)
FLOUR, TO COAT

120 G (4¼ OZ), 2 CM (¾ INCH)
THICK SLICE KASSERI-STYLE
CHEESE, OR TALAGANI

LEMON QUARTERS,
TO SERVE

There is a typical pan called a saganaki which is used for cooking and serving this – a small pan with handles on either side. You can use kasseri, kefalotiri or a softer type of Greek cheese such as talagani, which is my favourite for this savoury version. Serve hot with lemon on the side for squeezing over.

Pour olive oil into a small non-stick frying pan to a depth of roughly 1 cm (½ inch).

Put the egg in one flat bowl and the flour in another. Heat up the oil. Dip the cheese slice in the egg, then pat it in the flour to coat well. Put the slice into the oil and fry until golden on both sides. Splash its sides with oil to make sure that they are fried golden too. The cheese must be crisp on the outside and softened on the inside. When done, remove the cheese from the pan with tongs and drain on paper towels. Serve hot, cut up into squares and with lemon juice squeezed over the top. If serving in the same dish, remove the cheese, pour away the oil, wipe the dish with a paper towel, return the cheese to the dish and squeeze some lemon over.

SAGANAKI WITH HONEY + SESAME

Σαγανάκι με μέλι και σουσάμι

SERVES 4

2 TABLESPOONS MILD HONEY

120 G (4¼ OZ), 2 CM (¾ INCH) THICK SLICES KASSERI CHEESE OR SIMILAR

1 EGG, LIGHTLY BEATEN

PLAIN (ALL-PURPOSE) FLOUR, TO COAT

LIGHT OLIVE OIL, FOR FRYING

1 TEASPOON BLACK SESAME SEEDS

This sweet saganaki seems to work better with a stronger cheese, so rather kasseri than talagani. This is also served as an appetiser and is a nice surprise among other savoury dishes, or just alone with a salad. I ate it on the island of Naxos.

Put the honey in a small briki (Greek coffee pot) or small saucepan and heat gently. Keep warm over a low heat.

Make the saganaki following the recipe on page 118. Serve the slice with some warm honey drizzled over and the sesame seeds sprinkled on top. Nice with bread, too.

KEFTEDES FRIED MEATBALLS

Κεφτέδες

MAKES ABOUT 35

300 G (10½ OZ) UNPEELED
POTATOES, (ABOUT 2)

500 G (1 LB 2 OZ) MINCED
BEEF

1 RED ONION, GRATED

2 TABLESPOONS COARSELY
CHOPPED FLAT-LEAF
PARSLEY

1 TEASPOON DRIED
OREGANO

1 TEASPOON DRIED MINT

GOOD PINCH OF GROUND
CINNAMON

1 EGG, LIGHTLY BEATEN

PLAIN (ALL-PURPOSE)
FLOUR, FOR DUSTING

OLIVE OIL, FOR FRYING

LEMON QUARTERS,
FOR SERVING

These are very popular in Greece. They are lovely as a meze with a dish of feta and a few other bits and pieces. Of course they are also great with chips. Many Greeks roll their keftedes in a little flour before frying.

Boil the potatoes, covered, in plenty of water until they are soft when pierced with a fork.

Meanwhile, put the beef, onion, parsley, oregano, mint, cinnamon and egg into a bowl and mix through. Drain the cooked potatoes and when they are cool enough to handle, peel and break up into the bowl. Season well with salt and pepper then mash everything together with a potato masher. Knead again with your hands to make a compact mix. Form walnut-sized balls of about 25 g (1 oz) but you can make them smaller or bigger if you like. Scatter some flour onto a flat plate and roll the balls lightly in the flour, keeping them in compact balls.

Heat olive oil to a depth of about ½ cm (¼ inch) in a large non-stick frying pan. Add as many balls as will fit to the pan and fry until they are golden on all sides, flicking them gently to roll over.

You will probably have to fry in 2 batches. Remove carefully with tongs and drain on a plate lined with paper towels. Add a little salt (as fried things are always good with a last sprinkling of salt). Serve hot, with a few drops of lemon juice.

REVITHOKEFTEDES CHICKPEA BALLS

Ρεβυθοκεφτέδες

MAKES 18

110 G (3¾ OZ/½ CUP) DRIED CHICKPEAS

1 TABLESPOON PLAIN (ALL-PURPOSE) FLOUR, PLUS EXTRA, FOR DUSTING

180 G (6½ OZ) POTATO (1 MEDIUM–LARGE), WASHED

40 G (1½ OZ) ONION, GRATED ON THE LARGE HOLES OF A GRATER

1 TABLESPOON COARSELY CHOPPED DILL

1 TABLESPOON COARSELY CHOPPED FLAT-LEAF PARSLEY

LIGHT OLIVE OIL, FOR FRYING

LEMON QUARTERS, TO SERVE

These are everywhere on the island of Sifnos and go well on any table with anything, anywhere at any time. The chickpeas are not cooked here, only soaked overnight and then pulsed to a purée in a food processor. Leave a little texture in them though.

Soak the chickpeas and the flour in plenty of cold water overnight.

Boil the potato in salted water until very tender. Drain. When cool enough to handle, peel and mash with a fork in a large bowl. Drain the soaked chickpeas and purée them, leaving some texture. Add to the potato along with the onion, dill and parsley. Season with salt and pepper and mix well. Shape 18 walnut-sized balls of about 25 g (1 oz)

each. Put some flour in a bowl and gently roll the balls in this to coat.

Pour the olive oil into a large frying pan to a depth of 5 mm (¼ inch) and put over a medium–high heat.

Fry the balls in batches, gently turning them to brown evenly. As they are done, remove with tongs and drain on paper towels. Sprinkle with salt and serve hot or cold with the lemon quarters.

TOMATOKEFTEDES FRIED TOMATO BALLS

Ντοματοκεφτέδες

MAKES ABOUT 15

300 G (10½ OZ) LOVELY RIPE
RED TOMATOES (ABOUT 3)

70 G (2½ OZ, 1 SMALL) RED
ONION, ROUGHLY CHOPPED

3 HEAPED TABLESPOONS
ROUGHLY CHOPPED MINT

100 G (3½ OZ/1⅔ CUP) PLAIN
ALL-PURPOSE FLOUR

1 HEAPED TEASPOON
BAKING POWDER

OLIVE OIL, FOR FRYING

These are everywhere on the island of Santorini. Santorini will offer you amazing tomatoes, fava, capers, wine, seafood, views, volcanoes ... if you go slightly out of season, it is incredible. Some go just for the sunset, dangling legs off walls towards the departing star and its spectacular performance. You may have to go there to get your tomatoes to make these lovely fried things. Alternatively choose wonderful ripe red tomatoes. These have lovely rough edges, bits of tomato, mint or onion chunks sticking out of the sides that have frozen during the frying like hedgehogs.

Cut the top hats off the unpeeled tomatoes and discard. Slice the tomatoes into 6 wedges then chop each wedge into 4 or 5 pieces. Scrape off the board into a bowl but leave behind the excess juice. Add the onion, mint and half the flour to the bowl. Season with salt and pepper and knead in well. Leave for 10 minutes or so to soften.

Make a paste with the remaining flour, the baking powder and 80 ml (2½ fl oz/⅓ cup) of water. Add to the bowl and mix in well. Heat olive oil to a depth of about 1.5 cm (⅝ inch) in a large non-stick frying pan until very hot. Scoop up a good tablespoon of the mixture and with another spoon, scrape this into the hot oil in lovely irregular fritters. Fry a few at a time, turning them over when golden to fry the other side. Remove with a slotted spoon and drain on a plate lined with paper towels. Sprinkle with a little extra salt and serve on a clean plate.

KOLOKITHAKIA KE MELITZANES TIGANITES FRIED MARROW + AUBERGINE

Κολοκυθάκια και μελιτζάνες τηγανιτές

SERVES 3

1 ZUCCHINI (MARROW)
(ABOUT 200 G/7 OZ)

½ EGGPLANT (AUBERGINE)
(ABOUT 200 G/7 OZ), HALVED
LENGTHWAYS

PLAIN (ALL-PURPOSE)
FLOUR, FOR COATING

LIGHT OLIVE OIL,
FOR FRYING

ALATOPIPERIGANO
(PAGE128)

TZATZIKI (PAGE130)

The wonderful thing I learned in Greece in the summer was this quick twice flouring and dipping in water method that produces a great crispier result. So have a bowl of flour and a bowl of cold water ready. It may seem like a bit of a fuss but it's worth it. This is a beauty with tzatziki for dipping the fried vegetables into.

Cut the zucchini into slices of about 3 mm (⅛ inch) thick. Cut the eggplant into half-moons of about 3 mm (⅛ inch) thick. Put the flour onto a plate, and have a bowl of cold water ready

Pour the olive oil into a large non-stick frying pan to roughly 1 cm (½ inch) deep and heat. Pat slices of zucchini in flour to coat both sides. Shake off the excess then dip the slices in the water. Shake a bit and pat well in flour again on both sides. Fry in batches until golden, turning them over and frying the other side too. Don't overcrowd the pan and if they're cooking too quickly, then turn the heat down. Remove the crisp and golden zucchini slices to a large plate lined with paper towels. Scatter them with alatopiperigano and get the next batch going. Once the zucchini are done, do the exact same thing with the eggplant. Serve hot, with tzatziki. These are also lovely with lemon.

ALATOPIPERIGANO
ALATI=SALT
PIPERI=PEPPER
RIGANI=OREGANO

Αλατοπιπερίγανο

1 TEASPOON SALT

2 TEASPOONS DRIED OREGANO

FEW GRINDS OF BLACK PEPPER

———

It is easy to scatter these ingredients over separately, but you can also mix them up to have ready for scattering over fried and grilled food. Needless to say, it's wonderful over chips. Also with some grilled bread draped with olive oil and some of this, as a snack, or on the side of any meal. Mix all together and keep in an airtight jar.

PATATES TIGANITES CHIPS

Πατάτες τηγανιτές

SERVES 2

2 LONG POTATOES
(ABOUT 300 G/10½ OZ)

LIGHT OLIVE OIL,
FOR FRYING

ALATOPIPERIGANO
(SEE OPPOSITE)

This amount of chips is just small enough to make a flat layer in the pan and not be too crowded and yet enough to make it worth the extra trouble of making chips. They are great with tzatziki (page 130). Chips are also wonderful with some feta crumbled over them and then a crumbling of dried oregano. Chips in Greece are often served next to a main saucy dish with a scattering of grated cheese over.

Peel the potatoes, halve them lengthways and slice each half into 3 or 4 gondolas. Put into a bowl of cold water with some salt and leave them for 30 minutes–1 hour to soak off some of the starch. Drain well and pat dry with paper towel. Wrap in a clean tea towel to dry further while the oil is heating.

Pour a good 1 cm (½ inch) depth of oil into a large frying pan and heat. When you think it's hot enough, throw in a chip to see if it bubbles and fizzles. If so, add all the chips, levelling them so they are not on top of each other. When they start to look soft, poke at them with a wooden spoon to roughen up their surfaces. Leave them alone again until they start looking crunchy, then shuffle them with a wooden spoon, turning them if necessary. Turn the heat down if the oil bubbles too quickly and becomes too hot, you don't want dark brown, soggy chips. When they are light golden and crisp, move them around in the pan with a slotted spoon and remove to a plate lined with paper towels. Scatter with alatopiperigano. Serve at once.

TZATZIKI YOGHURT, CUCUMBER, GARLIC

Τζατζίκι

MAKES A NICE BOWLFUL

2 GARLIC CLOVES

1 TABLESPOON OLIVE OIL

1 SMALL CUCUMBER
(160 G/5¾ OZ)

1 TEASPOON SALT

350 G (12 OZ) GREEK
YOGHURT

1½ TABLESPOONS
CHOPPED MINT

This is a subtle amount of garlic compared with some versions that you may come across. So you can add more if you like. If the garlic bothers you, you can leave it out completely, but it's not really tzatziki then. (And, garlic is good for colds plus it keeps vampires away.) See Yoghurt on the side (opposite) for a plainer version. Tzatziki is a beauty as it takes just about anything to a different level. Wonderful with chips, lamb chops, bread and many other dishes.

You can use 2 teaspoons or so of dried mint instead of fresh. If you prefer a milder garlic taste, then marinate the garlic in the oil and pour off the oil after without adding the garlic. If you are making regular tzatziki, then just make sure everyone within a five mile radius has some.

Using the flat of your knife, crush the garlic with a pinch of salt into a paste. Put into a small bowl with the oil and leave to marinate while you proceed with the rest.

Top and tail the cucumber, and peel it. I like it striped, with one strip peeled and the next left unpeeled. Using the large holes of the grater, grate the cucumber into a sieve. Scatter with the salt and leave it for 30 minutes or so to drain, turning it over a couple of times and even squashing it down with your hands or a wooden spoon.

Put the yoghurt into a bowl for serving. Add the garlic and oil, the mint and a couple of grinds of black pepper. Fold the cucumber through and taste for salt. This can be stored in the fridge, covered, for a couple of days. The cucumber will give up a little water but stir it through to loosen the tzatziki.

YIAOURTI YOGHURT ON THE SIDE

Γιαούρτι

SERVES 4 TO 6

1 GARLIC CLOVE, SQUASHED

1 TABLESPOON OLIVE OIL

250 G (9 OZ/1 CUP) GREEK YOGHURT

ROUGHLY 60 G (2¼ OZ/ ¼ CUP) PLAIN YOGHURT

A LARGE PINCH OF PAPRIKA

½ TEASPOON DRIED MINT

Of course a good dollop of plain thick Greek yoghurt, unfussed with, is also wonderful. For example, on a baked potato with a drizzling of olive oil and a scattering of salt and pepper.

This works very well in place of tzatziki for dishes where you may want something plainer. Depending on what you will be serving it with you can leave out the mint and paprika.

Put the squashed garlic and the olive oil in a cup and leave to steep for half an hour or so.

Put the Greek yoghurt in a bowl. Add just enough regular

yoghurt to loosen it (you might have some left over as not all Greek yoghurts are of the same thickness). Add the paprika and mint, and pour the olive oil in, keeping back the garlic clove. Season to taste with salt and black pepper and mix through.

HTAPODI XIDATO VINEGARED OCTOPUS

Χταπόδι ξυδάτο

SERVES 4 TO 6

1 LARGE OCTOPUS (ABOUT 1.2 KG/2 LB 10 OZ)

6 TABLESPOONS OLIVE OIL

6 TABLESPOONS RED WINE VINEGAR

½ TEASPOON DRIED OREGANO

1 LARGE GARLIC CLOVE, CHOPPED

This is a wonderful meze served with ouzo or raki.

There is a saying in some parts of Greece that says 'the octopus separates the couple', as it appears so big initially and ends up so shrunk when cooked. Years ago when the husband saw the result after a hard day's work he might have been furious with his wife that there was much less to eat than what had appeared in the uncooked state!

You will often see octopus catchers in Greece bashing their just caught octopus against the rocks to tenderise.

To prepare the octopus, slice about two-thirds of the way across, just below the eyes, keeping the tentacles still attached to the head. Scrape the innards out of the head, being careful not to puncture the ink sac. Cut the hard eyes from the head and push the beak out from the centre of the tentacles. Rinse under cold running water and shake dry over the sink. Put whole into a heavy-based pot with absolutely nothing else. Cover, put over the lowest possible heat and simmer gently for about 1¼ hours, turning it a couple of times. It should stew in its own juices, but if it is looking dry and beginning to stick to the pot, add a little hot water. By the end, the liquid will be almost jammy and the octopus should be very tender when poked with a fork. If not, add a little more water and continue cooking.

Remove the pot from the heat and set aside, still covered, while

HTAPODI SCHARA GRILLED OCTOPUS

Χταπόδι σχάρας

the octopus cools down. Remove the octopus from the pot and slice away the tentacles. Cut the tentacles up into easy-to-put-on-your-fork pieces, discarding any skin that comes away. Put into a bowl and add the olive oil, vinegar, oregano, garlic, pepper, and taste for salt. Mix through. It is important that you can taste the vinegar – that's the name of this dish. Cover with plastic wrap and leave in the fridge to marinate for a few hours, turning it through a couple of times, before serving.

A grilled octopus is equally excellent. Often these are cleaned and hung out in the sun to dry for a few hours. Sometimes they are boiled first to soften and then quickly grilled for flavour.

Prepare your octopus as opposite. Cut into 8 individual tentacles, and cut the head to open it out. Put the pieces in a wire grill rack and grill quickly over very hot coals, flipping them over when deep golden and charred here and there.

Cut up into good slices. Drizzle with olive oil, splash with red wine vinegar, crumble over some oregano and give a good grind of pepper. Serve with ouzo on ice.

GAVROS MARINATED ANCHOVIES

Γαύρος

SERVES 4 TO 6

300 G (10½ OZ) GAVROS (ANCHOVIES)

ABOUT 125 ML (4 FL OZ/ ½ CUP) WHITE WINE VINEGAR

1 HEAPED TABLESPOON CHOPPED FLAT-LEAF PARSLEY

3 TABLESPOONS OLIVE OIL, PLUS EXTRA FOR SERVING

2 GARLIC CLOVES, HALVED

1 TEASPOON DRIED OREGANO

JUICE OF ½ LEMON

You can add in some other herbs and spices here to take on a different flavour. This is great served with other fish meze like the vinegared octopus, and with some taramosalata and bread it can end up being the whole meal. The gavros will keep for 3 days or so, covered with plastic wrap in the fridge.

Cut the heads off the anchovies and run a small sharp knife down their bellies to open them out. Pull out the innards and the skeleton with the tail attached. If they haven't parted already, pull apart the sides to give 2 individual fillets. Rinse, then pat dry with paper towels. Arrange the fillets skin side down in a non-metallic dish which is just large enough to take them in 2 layers. Pour in enough vinegar to cover the fillets. Cover with plastic wrap and leave in the fridge for 4 hours or so.

Take the fillets from the dish, shaking off excess vinegar. Layer them in a flattish bowl, salting a little in between layers as you go. Add the parsley, olive oil and garlic, and the oregano crushed between your fingers to drop into the bowl. Add the lemon juice and a few good grinds of pepper. Shuffle to distribute. Cover with plastic wrap and leave to mingle before eating them – a few hours is good, the next day is even better. Drizzle with the extra olive oil just before eating.

GARIDES SAGANAKI PRAWNS WITH FETA + TOMATO

Γαρίδες σαγανάκι

SERVES 6 TO 8

ABOUT 16 MEDIUM PRAWNS

5 TABLESPOONS OLIVE OIL

50 G (1¾ OZ) ROUND SPRING ONIONS WITH SOME GREEN, FINELY CHOPPED

3 GARLIC CLOVES, CHOPPED

1 X 400 G (14 OZ) TIN CRUSHED TOMATOES

4 TABLESPOONS CHOPPED FLAT-LEAF PARSLEY

125 G (4½ OZ) FETA, CRUMBLED

I have seen these baked as well as made on the stovetop. This recipe has lovely strong, clean flavours and it works well as a meze with other seafood dishes. You really just need some bread with it.

Here I have cleaned the prawns leaving the tail on, but you might decide to leave the shell on, just cutting down the back and deveining.

Peel the prawns, leaving the tails intact, and devein them using a toothpick. Heat the oil in a wide non-stick pot that has a lid and sauté the onion on low–medium heat until softened. Add the garlic and fry until it smells good, then add the tomato, half the parsley and some salt and pepper. Put the lid on and simmer for 10 minutes or so.

Add the prawns to the pot and turn through to cover all of them with sauce. Simmer, covered, for 3 to 4 minutes. Scatter the feta in, put the lid back on and cook until the feta just softens, about 5 minutes, rocking the pot once or twice. Serve with a good grind of pepper and the remaining parsley scattered on top, and some lovely Greek bread.

KALAMARI TIGANITO FRIED CALAMARI

Καλαμάρι τηγανιτό

SERVES 2

400 G (14 OZ) SMALL–MEDIUM CALAMARI

PLAIN (ALL-PURPOSE) FLOUR, FOR DUSTING

LIGHT OLIVE OIL, FOR FRYING

ALATOPIPERIGANO (PAGE 128), TO SERVE

LEMON QUARTERS, TO SERVE

Please use lovely fresh and tender calamari here. It must be eaten with just a scattering of salt, pepper and oregano, and some lemon on the side for whoever would like. Have a bowl of plain flour and a bowl of water ready and your pan of oil heating up. Sometimes calamari splatters and pops in the pan, so it's a good idea to have a splatter mat that you can cover the pan with while the calamari are frying.

Cut the heads off and pull the innards from the calamari. Pull the transparent spine out of the body. Cut off the tentacles just above the eyes. Rinse the bodies and tentacles in cold water and dry them on paper towels. Slice the bodies into rings of about 1½ cm (⅝ inch) or as you like them. Keep the tentacles whole (unless they are big).

Put the flour on a deep plate, and pour cold water into a deep bowl. Pour olive oil to a depth of at least 1 cm (½ inch) into a frying pan and put over a high heat. Pat the calamari in the flour to coat well, shake off the excess then quickly dip them in the cold water. Pat them again well in the flour and shake off lightly. Fry in batches in the hot oil, turning them once, until they are golden and crusty. Remove to a plate lined with paper towels to drain while frying the rest. Scatter the lot with alatopiperigano and serve at once with lemon for those who would like it.

TIROKAFTERI SPICY FETA

Τυροκαυτερή

MAKES ROUGHLY 1 CUP

1 GARLIC CLOVE

2 TABLESPOONS OLIVE OIL

2 MILD GREEN CHILLIES (ABOUT 20 G/¾ OZ EACH)

240 G (8¾ OZ) FETA, BROKEN INTO SMALLISH PIECES

OLIVE OIL, TO SERVE

A PINCH OR 2 OF GROUND CHILLI, ACCORDING TO TASTE

This is great with koulouria bread rings (or regular bread or pita), as part of a meze or even just alone. I love it served before grilled lemon and oregano lamb chops with a plate of plain stewed green beans, a green salad and a dish of olives. Very fine. You can make it hotter or milder as you like – naturally this will depend on your chillies. Will keep in the fridge, covered, for 5 to 6 days.

Preheat the oven to the hottest it will go. Peel the garlic and bruise it with the flat of your knife and put it into a small bowl with the olive oil to steep. Trim and de-seed the chillies. It's a good idea to use disposable gloves for this, so the burning chilli doesn't remain on your hands. Put them on a sheet of foil and dry roast them in the oven for about 10 minutes, until soft and blistery. Chop them up finely then put in a mortar or mini processor with a tablespoon of the oil and blend to a paste. Add the feta and pulse until all the lumps are gone.

Scrape into a bowl and stir in the olive oil minus the garlic. Serve with a little olive oil dribbled over and a sprinkling of ground chilli if you think it's not hot enough.

PIPERIES XIDATES MARINATED PEPPERS

Πιπεριές ξυδάτες

The lovely small sweet Greek peppers can be fried whole or grilled, their skins removed then put in a dish to marinate with a little vinegar, salt and oregano, a clove of garlic and a splash of best olive oil. They are fantastic with mashed feta on bread and some olives. These will keep in the fridge, covered with plastic wrap, for a few days, but they are best eaten at room temperature.

CUCUMBER MEZE

Αγγουρομεζές

SERVES 2

1 CUCUMBER (ABOUT 200 G/
7 OZ), PEELED, SLICED

JUICE OF ½ LEMON

½ TEASPOON DRIED MINT

ABOUT 1 TABLESPOON OLIVE
OIL

This is extremely instant and extremely simple. The kind of thing you could eat a bucket of in summer. The recipe is easy to double; just reduce the olive oil slightly – about 1½ tablespoons.

Put the cucumber and lemon juice into a bowl and crumble the mint in. Add salt and pepper. Drizzle the olive oil over just before serving.

PIPERIES YEMISTES ME FETA PEPPERS STUFFED WITH FETA

Πιπεριές (γεμιστές) με φέτα

SERVES 4

4 SMALL RED AND GREEN
SWEET PEPPERS, ABOUT
40 G (1½ OZ) EACH AND
10 CM (4 INCHES) LONG

200 G (7 OZ) FETA

1 TABLESPOON OLIVE OIL

¼ TEASPOON DRIED
OREGANO, OPTIONAL

Greek florinis, red peppers, are beautiful and sweet. And they also have pale green thin-fleshed ones which are ideal for this dish. Very different in size to the large round capsicums (peppers) available in many places. You will need something like the long thin ones which weigh around 40 g (1½ oz) each. You could also use mizithra in place of the feta.

Cut the tops off the peppers and carefully remove the seeds, keeping the peppers whole. Crumble the feta and stuff tightly into the peppers, then replace the tops. Heat the olive oil in a frying pan and sauté the peppers over high heat (propping the peppers up against the sides of the pan so the filling doesn't ooze out), gently turning them over, until they are lightly browned on the outside, and the feta is melted a bit but not running out (the hats may fall off but replace when serving). Serve whole or cut into thick slices, with the oregano crumbled over the top.

FETA FOURNOU BAKED FETA

Φέτα φούρνου

•

SERVES 2, OR 4 AS PART
OF A MEZE

200 G (7 OZ) FETA,
CRUMBLED

1 SMALL GREEN SWEET
PEPPER, FINELY SLICED
ABOUT 40 G (1½ OZ)

½ SMALL TOMATO, CHOPPED

1 TO 2 TABLESPOONS
OLIVE OIL

2 GOOD PINCHES OF DRIED
OREGANO

This is nice made in small individual ceramic dishes. Mine are flat and about 11 cm (4¼ inches) in diameter and 3 cm (1¼ inches) high.

Serve hot with bread.

Preheat the oven to 200°c (400°f/gas 6). Divide the feta between 2 small shallow ceramic dishes. Scatter the green pepper over the top and then the tomato over the pepper. Drizzle on the olive oil, crumble the oregano in and top with a good grind of black pepper. Bake until a bit crusty on the sides, about 20 minutes.

MELITZANOSALATA MASHED AUBERGINE

Μελιτζανοσαλάτα

SERVES 6

1 LARGE EGGPLANT (AUBERGINE) ABOUT 350 G/ 12 OZ, PREFERABLY LONG, NOT ROUND

2 TABLESPOONS OLIVE OIL

½ SMALL RED ONION, PEELED AND FINELY CHOPPED

1 GARLIC CLOVE, PEELED AND FINELY CHOPPED

1 SMALL TOMATO (ABOUT 50 G/1¾ OZ), PEELED AND CHOPPED, NOT TOO FINELY

2 TEASPOONS LEMON JUICE

¼ TEASPOON SWEET PAPRIKA

½ TEASPOON DRIED OREGANO

1 HEAPED TABLESPOON ROUGHLY CHOPPED FLAT-LEAF PARSLEY

If you have a barbecue going at the same time, then it is wonderful to grill your eggplant on it. If not, you can roast it on a high temperature in the oven to darken the skin in places and give it a lovely smoky roasted taste. It is important to dry out the eggplant, to get the flesh soft and scrapable and not liquidy.

There are many different versions of this eggplant dish; some have vinegar rather than the lemon juice, others have yoghurt. You could also add some fresh mint for a different journey. Lovely with pita as a meze or alone even. Or as a side next to a lamb dish.

Preheat the barbecue to hot. Rinse the eggplant then prick it in a few places here and there with a fork so the skin won't burst while cooking. Put it on a rack 15 cm (6 inches) or so from the coals and grill for 40 to 50 minutes, turning a few times until softened, blackened and smoky. Set aside to cool slightly.

While the eggplant is cooking, heat the olive oil in a non-stick frying pan and sauté the onion until sticky and well cooked, but not browned. Add the garlic and cook until you just smell it, then stir in the tomato. Simmer for 10 minutes or so, until the tomato has collapsed into a chunky sauce and you can see tomato frying in oil again. Remove from the heat.

Cut the stalk off the eggplant and halve the eggplant lengthways. Squeeze out excess liquid over the sink. Using a pointed teaspoon, scrape out the flesh into a bowl and mash or chop it finely. Discard the skin. Add the tomato mixture and mash it roughly with a fork. Add the lemon juice, paprika and herbs and season with salt and pepper. Serve at room temperature.

MIDIA MUSSELS WITH FETA + PEPPERS

Μύδια

SERVES 6 OR SO

ABOUT 1.5 KG (3 LB 5 OZ)
BLACK MUSSELS

5 TABLESPOONS OLIVE OIL

1 SMALL RED SWEET
PEPPER (ABOUT 40 G/1½ OZ)
SLICED INTO THIN RINGS

1 SMALL GREEN SWEET
PEPPER (ABOUT 40 G/1½ OZ)
SLICED INTO THIN RINGS

2 GARLIC CLOVES, CHOPPED

PINCH OF GROUND CHILLI

JUICE OF 2 LEMONS

200 G (7 OZ) FETA,
ROUGHLY CHOPPED

4 TABLESPOONS CHOPPED
FLAT-LEAF PARSLEY

The Greek peppers are beautiful. Red and pale green. Small and long. Thin fleshed. A couple of them here sliced in rings give a great flavour. If you can't find those then use a similar weight of other small sweet peppers.

This dish can also be served with the mussels shelled, but I love shells on. Make sure your mussels are fresh. Serve with bread.

De-beard the mussels. Scrub them with a wire brush under cold running water, then drain. Give each one a tap and discard those which stay open. Heat the oil in a pot large enough to take the mussels and which has a lid. Sauté the peppers until softened. Add the garlic and chilli and when it smells good, add the mussels. Put the lid on, turn up the heat and cook just a minute or so until the mussels open Give the ones that haven't opened another chance to open, but then discard those that still have not opened. Add the lemon juice, put the lid back on and give the pan a shake.

Scatter the feta over the top, return the lid and shake the pan again. Leave for a minute for the feta to soften but don't let it dissolve, it's nice to be able to see soft chunks of feta here and there. Add the parsley and a good few grinds of black pepper and turn the mussels through gently. Serve hot.

OMELETA HORIATIKI POTATO, FETA + OREGANO OMELETTE

Ομελέτα χωριάτικη

SERVES 4

4 TABLESPOONS OLIVE OIL

300 G (10½ OZ) POTATOES, PEELED, CUT INTO 4 MM (⅛ INCH) ROUNDS

1 TEASPOON DRIED OREGANO

100 G (3½ OZ) FETA

6 EGGS, LIGHTLY BEATEN

This, served with bread and a salad, is a wonderfully simple supper. It is ideal if you can have the oven grill on to finish cooking the large omelette by giving heat from the top, but if not, then just continue cooking it covered on low on the stovetop.

Heat the oil in a 28 cm (11¼ inch) non-stick frying pan. Add the potatoes and fry gently on both sides until golden (but not too crisp), and completely cooked through. Salt lightly. Crumble the oregano over the potato with your fingers, then crumble the feta on top.

If you have a grill (broiler), preheat it now to hot. Pour the egg into the pan, shuffling gently so that it can leak down and around the potato. Put the lid on and cook over low heat until the egg is set throughout but still runny on top. Keep an eye on the heat to ensure that the bottom doesn't burn but forms a golden crust. Take the lid off the pan and place the pan 10 cm (4 inches) or so under the grill. If you aren't using a grill, just keep the lid on the pan and continue cooking the egg slowly. When it's just slightly runny here and there, remove from the heat and leave it with the lid on for a couple of minutes. Loosen the edges and slide it out of the pan upright onto a large serving plate. Serve hot, with a grind of black pepper.

STRAPATSADA SCRAMBLED EGGS WITH TOMATO

Στραπατσάδα

SERVES 3

2 TABLESPOONS OLIVE OIL

½ SMALL RED ONION, THINLY SLICED

500 G (1 LB 2 OZ) RIPE TOMATOES, PEELED, CHOPPED

3 EGGS

DRIED OREGANO

This is something very simple that Greeks love to eat. Serve with some country-style bread, a dish of olives, and a dish of feta.

Heat the oil in a large non-stick frying pan and sauté the onion until it begins to soften. Add the tomatoes and season with salt. Simmer for a few minutes to reduce, but leave some chunkiness. Break the eggs in, leave them for a bit until they start to set, then push them through the tomatoes with a wooden spoon until just cooked. Serve at once with a grind of pepper and a crumbling of oregano.

BAKER'S

FOODS

The yayia's (grandmother's) face in the bakery on the island of Lipsi broke into many more smiling creases as she saw the children. Her spontaneous arm stretched through the heavenly baker's air, past the spinach pies, cheese pies, all the other pies, and the huge round pillows of breads until it landed on a sweet roll, which she broke in half for the children. The pure generosity and kindness that exists in so many of the older-faced generation who have eaten healthy food all their lives. And testimony to the fact that children in Greece are highly considered. There seems no problem about your child tearing around the avli (courtyard) of a restaurant with other children they have just found. No need to apologise, or pretend that your children are normally far calmer than this.

PITA BREAD

Πίτα

MAKES 8 PITA BREADS

14 G (½ OZ) FRESH YEAST
OR 2 TEASPOONS (7 G/⅛ OZ)
DRIED

1 TEASPOON HONEY

450 G (1 LB/3 CUPS) BREAD
(STRONG) FLOUR

6 TABLESPOONS OLIVE OIL

Generally in Greece pita is found at a souvlaki house (souvlatzithiko) and some grill places. But it is also wonderful served plain instead of bread at your table with dips etc.

In Greece, the pita are more often wrapped than stuffed for souvlaki and kebabs, so they need to be a bit softer. They are then heated up on the barbecue, or in the oven or chargrill (griddle) pan before filling. If you will be eating them straight away, however, cook them a little longer, until they just start to colour. These can be frozen once cooked and then just pulled out to thaw.

Crumble the fresh yeast or sprinkle the dried yeast into a large wide bowl – the same one that will hold your dough later for rising.

Add the honey and 3 tablespoons of warm water and mix to dissolve. Leave it till it starts to activate and get frothy. Add 1 heaped teaspoon of salt, the flour, oil and an extra 200 ml (7 fl oz) of water to the dough and mix with a wooden spoon until a rough dough clumps around it. Change to your hands and knead until you have a soft springy dough, 8 to 10 minutes. It will seem sticky at first but that is good, so only add more flour if the dough clings to your hands.

Wipe out the bowl with an oiled paper towel. Put the dough in, cover with plastic wrap then a heavy cloth and leave in a warm place until it has puffed up and almost doubled in size, 1½ to 2 hours.

159

Preheat the oven to 200°c (400°f/gas 6). Knock the dough down and divide it into 8 balls about 100 g (3½ oz) each. Press each ball into a flat disc with your hand and leave for 5 minutes for them to relax.

Roll the discs out with a rolling pin to a circle of about 6 cm (2½ inches) diameter and about 2 mm (¹⁄₁₆ inch) thick. Brush lightly with olive oil and put onto unfloured baking trays. Bake one tray at a time until they are firmed on the first side, 5 minutes or so, then turn them over and bake for another 3 minutes, or until the top surface is dry. You will finish cooking them under the grill (broiler) or in the oven when about to serve, so they should be a little under-done at this stage. Remove and immediately stack them on top of each other and wrap in plastic wrap to keep them limp so you will be able to wrap them around your kebabs. Alternatively, you can fry each bread in a hot dry frying pan until just changed colour but not browned, about 1 minute each side. Stack and wrap in plastic wrap as you go.

To serve, brush each side lightly with olive oil and put under the grill to warm both sides, or use a hot chargrill (griddle) pan.

KOULOURIA SESAME BREAD RINGS

Κουλούρια

MAKES 12

25 G (1 OZ) FRESH YEAST, OR 14 G (½ OZ/1 TABLESPOON) DRIED

PINCH OF SUGAR

300 ML (10½ FL OZ) LUKEWARM WATER

600 G (1 LB 5 OZ) BREAD (STRONG) FLOUR

1 TEASPOON SALT

4 TABLESPOONS OLIVE OIL

ABOUT 150 G (5½ OZ) SESAME SEEDS

FLOUR PASTE

3 TEASPOONS BREAD (STRONG) FLOUR

3 TABLESPOONS WATER

Koulouri means 'coil' in Greece. I adore these for breakfast. Or with tarama or tirokafteri later on. They sometimes differ in size, but generally are round, a bit flattened and slightly irregular in shape. These are sold on the streets by koulourades. The nice thing is that when you get them in a packet, many sesame seeds fall to the bottom, then you can pour them out and eat them off your hand.

Crumble the fresh yeast or sprinkle the dried into a bowl. Add the sugar, water and a handful of flour. Whisk to smooth any lumps. Leave until it starts to activate and bubble, about 10 minutes. Add the rest of the flour, the salt and oil and mix with a wooden spoon until a loose dough forms. Knead on a lightly floured surface for 7 to 8 minutes or until the dough is smooth and spongy. Wipe out the bowl with an oiled paper towel and put the dough in. Cover with plastic wrap then a tea towel and leave in a warm spot for about 2 hours until puffed and doubled in size.

Preheat the oven to 200°c (400°f/gas 6) and line 2 baking trays with baking paper. For the flour paste, mix the flour and water in a bowl until smooth. Knead the dough briefly then divide it into 12 equal parts. Roll, stretch and coax each piece into a thin rope about 40 cm (16 inches) long. Make the first 6 and while baking, prepare the next batch. Brush each rope lightly with the paste, and sprinkle sesame seeds all over, then roll through the seeds that have dropped on your work surface so that they're covered all over. Turn each rope on itself forming a ring, pressing the ends together to seal. Place on a tray and bake for 20 minutes or until golden. Sesame seeds which have fallen onto the trays can be used elsewhere.

ELIOPSOMO OLIVE BREAD

Ελιόψωμο

MAKES 1 LOAF

15 G (½ OZ) FRESH YEAST,
OR 7 G (¼ OZ/ 2 TEASPOONS)
DRIED

PINCH OF SUGAR

160 ML (5¼ FL OZ) WARM
WATER

300 G (10½ OZ) BREAD
(STRONG) FLOUR

½ TEASPOON SALT

1 TABLESPOON OLIVE OIL,
PLUS EXTRA FOR BRUSHING

60 G (2¼ OZ) DRAINED
PITTED KALAMATA OLIVES,
HALVED

1 TEASPOON DRIED
OREGANO

SMALL SPRIG OF DRIED
OREGANO, FOR THE TOP

A myth narrates how Athina became the protectress of the city of Athens. At the moment of the foundation of the city, two gods offered to protect it. Poseidon and Athina. It was decided that the inhabitants would choose the god with the most useful and precious gift. Poseidon struck the ground with his trident and a horse was born. He said: 'My gift is the horse, which will render you swifter and give you the strength to combat your enemies.' (Another myth claims he created a well from which water shot forth but was salty rendering it undrinkable.) Then it was Athina's turn. The goddess planted her staff into the ground and immediately it was transformed into a twisted tree with silver leaves, laden with small black fruits. The goddess said: 'My gift is the olive tree; the juice of its fruits will bring peace, health and prosperity to you and your table.' The inhabitants chose the gift of Athina. And dedicated the Parthenon to Athina as protectress of their city.

Most often olives in Greece are served just plain and are loved as they are. Apart from the generous handfuls that are tossed into salads, they are not used in cooking much.

Here is a lovely bread to use the wonderful Greek olives in. It's also good toasted.

Crumble the fresh or scatter the dried yeast into a large bowl. Add the sugar and water and leave it to activate and bubble. Add the flour, salt and olive oil and mix first with a wooden spoon, then your hands to get a soft dough. Knead for 8 to 10 minutes, until smooth and spongy. Wipe out the bowl with paper towels and put the dough in. Make a cross on the dough by pressing with the edge of your hand (to bless the dough). Cover the bowl with plastic wrap and then a tea towel and put in a warm spot for a couple of hours to rise.

Pat the olives dry with paper towels. Put them in a bowl with the oregano and toss well. When the dough has risen and is doubled in size, knead it again, this time working in the olives and oregano until they are evenly distributed.

You might need to use a little extra flour as the olives will add some oil to the dough. Shape into an oval loaf, making sure a few olives are showing on the outside. Put on a baking tray which has been lined with baking paper. Brush the bread with oil and if you have the sprig of oregano, press this onto the top. Cover with a cake net to keep the insects away and leave in a warm spot for about 1 hour to rise again.

In the meantime, preheat the oven to 200°c (400°f/gas 6). Bake the bread for about 30 minutes, until it is golden and sounds hollow when tapped on the base. Cool on a wire rack before slicing.

SPANAKOPITA SPINACH PIES

Σπανακόπιτα

MAKES 9

27 SHEETS OF PHYLLO PASTRY*, FINAL DIMENSIONS 23 X 25 CM (9 X 10 INCHES)

OLIVE OIL, FOR BRUSHING

FILLING

5 TABLESPOONS OLIVE OIL

180 G (6½ OZ/1½ CUPS) CHOPPED ROUND SPRING ONIONS WITH SOME GREEN

700 G (1 LB 9 OZ, ABOUT 2 BUNCHES) SPINACH LEAVES, WASHED, DRAINED, ROUGHLY SHREDDED

20 G (¾ OZ/⅓ CUP) COARSELY CHOPPED FRESH DILL (INCLUDE SOME STALKS)

200 G (7 OZ) FETA, COARSELY GRATED

2 EGGS, LIGHTLY BEATEN

FRESHLY GRATED NUTMEG

There are many variations on spinach pies in Greece involving different pastries and different fillings, some with feta and others just plain. This one has a little feta and uses phyllo pastry. These are delicious as a meal or snack.

You will need an oven dish of about 32 x 20 cm (12¾ x 8 inches) as you will arrange them in a long row.

To make the filling, choose a non-stick pot that is large enough to take all the spinach. Add the oil and put over medium heat. Add the onions and sauté until softened. Add the spinach and a little salt, and cook, covered, until the spinach wilts, turning it through a couple of times. Flick in a little water if necessary, but there should be enough coming from the spinach. Now uncover and simmer until the spinach softens and most of the water has evaporated. Remove to a bowl to cool. Add the dill, feta, egg, nutmeg and a few grinds of pepper. Mix thoroughly and taste a little for salt.

Preheat the oven to 180°c (350°f/gas 4) and grease a 32 x 20 cm (12¾ x 8 inch) ovenproof dish. Cut your phyllo sheets and keep them covered with a tea towel to prevent them drying out. Put the olive oil in a bowl. Now you will have to work quickly so that the pastry doesn't dry and crack, covering the phyllo you are not working with with a tea towel. Lay 1 phyllo sheet flat on a work surface and brush it well with olive oil. Lay another sheet neatly on top, brush it with oil and repeat once more, so that you have 3 layers. Now dollop 2 heaped tablespoons of filling along one short end, leaving a border of a couple of centimetres (inches). Drag the filling into an even line, then roll up the pastry fairly tightly into a cigar shape starting from the spinach end making one full turn, then turn and tuck the sides over and continue rolling. Brush the surface with oil. Make 8 more rolls in this way and as they are finished, arrange them in the dish side by side so they all fit touching in a row running from one short side to the opposite side, like soldiers all lined up. Bake for about 30 minutes or until golden. Cool a dash before serving as these are best eaten warm.

✿ The dimensions of commercial phyllo vary from brand to brand, so you will need to work out the number of phyllo sheets you require in the beginning, according to the maker's dimensions.

The geography of Greece must have added a lot to its specialness. So much coastline and so much sea with thousands of islands. It looks like a grand goddess was wading through the waters in a flowing dress and she rested her jewels down for a moment. Then time froze. And there they are – her jewels – grown towns with people in them. And she must be still watching over them.

TIROPITA CHEESE PIES

Τυρόπιτα

MAKES 9

27 SHEETS OF PHYLLO*
PASTRY*, FINAL
DIMENSIONS 23 X 25 CM
(9 X 10 INCHES)

OLIVE OIL, FOR BRUSHING

FILLING

450 G (1 LB) FETA, GRATED
COARSELY

200 G (7 OZ) RICOTTA

80 ML (2½ FL OZ/⅓ CUP)
MILK

You can brush the pastry with melted butter rather than the olive oil if you prefer. Great if your phyllo sheets are 50 cm (20 inches) long on one side, then you can cut two out of one, and the wastage is less. These are good served alone or with the spanakopita (page 168), then you can have one of each as a meal. Nice with a mixed salad.

To make the filling, put the feta, ricotta and milk in a bowl and mash all in well.

Preheat the oven to 180°c (350°f/gas 4) and grease a 32 x 20 cm (12¾ x 8 inch) ovenproof dish. Cut the phyllo sheets to size and keep them covered with a tea towel to prevent them drying out. Put some olive oil in a small bowl. Now you will have to work quickly so that the pastry doesn't dry and crack, covering the phyllo you are not working with with a tea towel. Lay 1 phyllo sheet flat on a work surface and brush it all over with olive oil. Lay another sheet neatly on top, brush it with oil and repeat once more, so that you have 3 layers. Spoon 2 unheaped tablespoons of filling along one short end, leaving a border of a couple of centimetres (inches). Drag the filling into an even line from one side to the other, then roll it up in the pastry fairly tightly, making one complete turn to

cover the feta, then tucking the sides
in and continuing to roll. Brush the
surface with oil. Make 8 more rolls
in this way and arrange them in the
dish side by side so they all fit in a
row running from one short side to
the opposite side, keeping seam sides
up so that leaks can stay on top.

Bake for about 30 minutes or
until golden. Cool a little before
serving as these are best eaten warm.

✿ The dimensions of commercial
phyllo vary from brand to brand,
so you will need to work out the
number of phyllo sheets you require
in the beginning, according to the
maker's dimensions.

TIROPITA ME ANITHO CHEESE PIE WITH DILL

Τυρόπιτα με άνιθο

SERVES MANY

150 G (5½ OZ/1 CUP) PLAIN (ALL-PURPOSE) FLOUR, PLUS A BIT EXTRA FOR ROLLING

¼ TEASPOON BAKING POWDER

1 TABLESPOON OLIVE OIL

60–125 ml (2–4 FL OZ/ ¼–½ CUP) WARM WATER

FILLING

250 G (9 OZ) FETA

250 G (9 OZ) ANTHOTIRO OR SOFT RICOTTA

1 TABLESPOON MILK

1 TABLESPOON OLIVE OIL

2 HEAPED TABLESPOONS COARSELY CHOPPED DILL

2 EGGS

This is a flat, salty feta pie with dill that Roulla, a lovely lady in Mani, taught me. She used one of those great coloured plastic bowls that you would do your hand washing in to mix her cheese, as she was making three times this amount for family and friends.

There is no salt in the pastry here because of the filling, so if you will be using the pastry for other purposes you can add a dash.

The dowel rod that many Greek housewives use as a rolling pin is very long and very thin and they are able to roll out their pastry paper-thin by wrapping it around this rod and rolling it together.

Preheat the oven to 170°c (325° f/ gas 3) and grease the base of a 28 cm (11¼ inch) pie dish or tin. Put the flour and baking powder into a basin. Add the olive oil and mix through, then start adding the water, enough to make a lovely soft dough. Knead until smooth, about a minute. Cover with plastic wrap and leave at room temperature for 20 minutes or so.

For the filling, coarsely grate the feta into a good large bowl. Grate the anthotiro also if using and add to the bowl, otherwise just add the ricotta. Mash it all together well. Add the milk, olive oil, dill and a good grind of pepper. Lightly whisk the eggs in a small bowl and pour all but a tablespoon in with the cheeses. Mix until well combined, if it seems stiff, thin it out with a little milk just to loosen up the mixture a bit, then cover and leave aside while you roll the dough.

Roll out the dough very thinly to a 1 to 2 mm (1/16 inch) circle of about 40 cm (16 inches) diameter. Drape it over your rolling pin or dowel rod, then lower it onto the pie dish, leaving the overhang for now. Scrape the filling mix on top and spread it evenly. Turn the pastry overhangs over the cheese mix so that you leave an uncovered area of about 5 cm (2 inches) in the middle. The pastry will be doubled over in places in an irregular way and that's how it is, but you can cut away a little where it's too thick. Brush the pastry with the remaining egg.

Bake in the oven until the bottom of the pastry is firm and the top is golden, about 40 minutes. Remove and cool a bit before cutting into thin slices. Good served warm or at room temperature.

HORTOPITA WILD GREENS PIE

Χορτόπιτα

MAKES ABOUT 35
DIAMONDS – SERVES A
COUPLE OF CLASSES

700 G (1 LB 9 OZ) LEAVES
OF MIXED WILD GREENS
(SUCH AS CHICORY (WITLOF),
MUSTARD GREENS OR
TURNIP GREENS) INCLUDING
SOME SPINACH

100 G (3½ OZ) ROUND
SPRING ONIONS, CHOPPED

30 G (1 OZ/½ CUP) CHOPPED
DILL

30 G (1 OZ/½ CUP) CHOPPED
FLAT-LEAF PARSLEY

¼ CUP CHOPPED FENNEL
FRONDS

300 G (10½ OZ) FETA,
CRUMBLED

OLIVE OIL, FOR BRUSHING

PASTRY

600 G (1 LB 5 OZ/4 CUPS)
PLAIN (ALL-PURPOSE)
FLOUR

1 TEASPOON BAKING
POWDER

4 TABLESPOONS OLIVE OIL

ABOUT 330 ML (11¼ FL OZ/
1⅓ CUPS) COLD WATER

This is from the principal of the elementary school, Hill, in Plaka Athens. Every year he makes it together with students and it is then distributed to the school. He says to make this, one needs 'meraki' (presence and heart, fun and patience). One should not consider the fact that the kitchen may be a mess afterwards on account of all the greens and flour everywhere. The pita he says, is a success if, when you cut it, it is dry, not oily or damp. Then you know you have done well. And this pita furthermore needs special music to succeed – klarino (clarinet), defi (frame drum), violi (violin) and laouto (lute), the classic Epirus band instruments. Only these, nothing else.

The original recipe is 7 layers of thinly rolled pastry, handfuls of wild poppy grass, stinging nettles, sorrel and 2 bunches of dill, and 3 handfuls of flour and various wild mountain grasses and leaves. You may mix in whatever of these you can find into the amount of greens given here, the wilder they are the more wonderful the flavour.

To make the pastry, put the flour and baking powder in a bowl with a big pinch of salt. Add the olive oil and stir in enough of the water to give a rough dough which clumps around your spoon. Now use your hands and knead the dough until smooth. Divide into 7 balls of about 135 g (4¾ oz) each and leave them to rest at room temperature while you make the filling.

For the filling, rinse the mixed leaves and drain in a colander. Chop coarsely and put in a big bowl. Add the spring onion, dill, parsley, fennel and feta, and season with a good amount of pepper and some salt (even though there is feta here it will still need about a teaspoon). Mix through very well. Preheat the oven to 180°c (350°f/gas 4) and brush the base and sides of a 36 cm (14¼ inch) round baking tin with olive oil. On a floured surface, roll out one of the pastry balls to the diameter of your baking tin. Because the pastry is so stretchy, you'll be able to pull it to fit, so just hold the tin over the rolled pastry to check that it's about the right size. Drape it over your rolling pin and lower it into the tin, stretching it if necessary to fit. Brush lightly with olive oil. Roll out another ball of pastry to cover the first. Brush with olive oil. Only the bottom of the pie will have a double layer of pastry.

Divide the filling into roughly 5 parts then scatter one-fifth over the pastry base. Roll out another pastry ball and now it is more manageable to brush it with olive oil before putting it over the greens. Scatter with another one-fifth of the greens and continue layering one

sheet of oiled pastry then a fifth of greens, finishing with a final pastry layer, making sure that it completely covers the greens. Neaten the edges by crimping the pastry or simply pushing any excess down the sides of the tin. Brush with olive oil. Bake for about 1 to 1¼ hours, until the top is crisp and golden.

Cool slightly before cutting into diamonds and serving.

CHANIOTIKO BOUREKI VEGETABLE PIE FROM CHANIA

Χανιώτικο Μπουρέκι

SERVES 12

300 G (10½ OZ) POTATOES, CUT INTO 3 MM (⅛ INCH) SLICES

750 G (1 LB 10 OZ) ZUCCHINI (COURGETTES), CUT INTO 3 MM (⅛ INCH) SLICES

2 TABLESPOONS CHOPPED MINT

2 TABLESPOONS CHOPPED FLAT-LEAF PARSLEY

500 G (1 LB 2 OZ) SOFT MIZITHRA OR RICOTTA

½ CUP GRATED KEFALOTIRI OR PARMESAN

1 EGG, LIGHTLY BEATEN

125 ML (4 FL OZ/½ CUP) OLIVE OIL

125 ML (4 FL OZ/½ CUP) MILK

60 G (2¼ OZ) PLAIN (ALL-PURPOSE) FLOUR

LARGE PINCH OF GRATED NUTMEG

1 LARGE RIPE TOMATO, PEELED, ROUGHLY CHOPPED

A friend of mine, Nikos, from Chania in northern Crete taught me this. If you can't find soft mizithra cheese you can use ricotta. Lovely layers of vegetables are first baked and then a pastry layer is added on and the pie is finished in the oven.

Preheat the oven to 180°c (350°f/gas 4). Put the vegetables, herbs, cheeses, the beaten egg, olive oil, milk, flour and nutmeg into a bowl. Add salt and a little pepper. Mix well with your hands, massaging it all together. Spread roughly three-quarters of the mix over the bottom of a 22 x 30 cm (8½ x 12 inch) ovenproof dish. Scatter the chopped tomatoes over this, then add the rest of the mix. Smooth the surface and poke holes through the mixture here and there with the end of a wooden spoon. Pour about 125 ml (4 fl oz/½ cup) of water into the emptied mixture bowl, swirl to rinse it then pour the water over the mixture in the dish, rocking it to distribute the water. Bake for about 45 minutes or until the vegetables are tender.

Meanwhile, make the pastry. Sift the flour and salt into a bowl. Mix in the olive oil and enough of the water to give a rough dough which clumps together. Knead until firm. Cover with plastic wrap and leave aside at room temperature.

Take the dish from the oven (leaving the oven on) when the vegetables are ready and set aside to cool a little.

Roll the dough out on a lightly floured surface to a rectangle slightly bigger than the dish size. It will be

very thin, just 1 to 2 mm (¹⁄₁₆ inch).
Rest it for a couple of minutes, then
fit it over the pie. Push down the
edges with a knife so that it curves
down the sides, or just fold the
pastry over to give a neat border.
Brush the surface with egg. Gently
cut through just the pastry into
12 portions. Sprinkle the top with
the sesame seeds and return to the
oven for about 20 minutes or so, until
the pastry is crisp and golden.

Cut into the pre-marked portions
and serve warm.

PASTRY

100 G (3½ OZ/²⁄₃ CUP) PLAIN
(ALL-PURPOSE) FLOUR

½ TEASPOON SALT

1 TABLESPOON OLIVE OIL

ABOUT 125ML (4 FL OZ/
½ CUP) WATER

1 EGG, LIGHTLY BEATEN,
FOR BRUSHING

1 HEAPED TEASPOON
SESAME SEEDS

SOUPS

Hurtling through the villages, along old, curled streets that cars these days can only just about get through. Past thick white walls that look like feta into places where time stops. Men go out for coffee and tavli (backgammon). Women are at home preparing food. Times gone from many places. And yet – a simplicity that many parts of Greece still tell us of.

KAKAVIA FISHERMAN'S SOUP

Κακαβιά

SERVES 4

1 KG (2 LB 4 OZ) ASSORTED WHOLE SOUP FISH, CLEANED AND GUTTED

A SMALL BUNCH OF FLAT-LEAF PARSLEY

⅓ STICK CELERY + 4 HEAPED TABLESPOONS CHOPPED INCLUDING SOME LEAVES

3 GARLIC CLOVES, 1 WHOLE, 2 CHOPPED

1 LARGE RED ONION

5 TABLESPOONS OLIVE OIL

60 ML (2 FL OZ/¼ CUP) WHITE WINE

450 G (14 OZ) VERY RIPE TOMATOES, PEELED, CUT INTO CHUNKS

400 G (1 LB) POTATOES, CUT INTO CHUNKS OF ABOUT 1.5 CM (⅝ INCH)

400 G (14 OZ) PERCH OR SNAPPER FILLET, CUT INTO 4 PIECES, OR 4 X 100 G (3½ OZ) FILLETS

JUICE OF 1 LEMON

2 HEAPED TABLESPOONS COARSELY CHOPPED FLAT-LEAF PARSLEY, TO SERVE

This is the type of chunky soup that a fisherman would make on his boat. Often the fish are left whole, but here I have first made a broth, strained it, and then cooked fillets of fish in it to avoid bones swimming around. It is so simple. Potatoes, onions, garlic, chunks of tomato and fish.

Make a broth. Put the soup fish into a stock pot and cover with 1 litre (35 fl oz/4 cups) of cold water. Add the bunch of parsley, piece of celery, whole garlic clove, salt and a couple of grinds of pepper. Peel the onion and cut off a piece from one side. Add this piece to the stock pot. Chop what's left of the onion and put to one side for the moment. Bring the pot to the boil. Lower the heat and simmer for about 20 minutes. Strain, discarding the bones and skin of the fish. You should have about 750 ml (26 fl oz/ 3 cups) of broth. Depending on the fish you've used, you may be able to salvage some flesh for another use.

Heat the oil in a large wide pot and sauté the chopped onion until softened and pale golden. Add the chopped celery and sauté until that softens too. Next add the chopped garlic and cook until you can smell it, then add the wine. Cook until the wine has almost evaporated then add the tomatoes, potatoes, some salt and pepper and simmer for about 5 minutes. Add the fish broth and simmer for another 5 minutes before adding the fillets. Lower the heat and simmer uncovered until it loses the watery look and the fish is cooked through, 10 minutes or so. Add the lemon juice and the extra chopped parsley, rock the pot to distribute it all gently and taste for salt. Add a grind of pepper and serve hot with bread.

PSAROSOUPA AVGOLEMONO EGG + LEMON FISH SOUP

Ψαρόσουπα αυγολέμονο

SERVES 4

1 KG (2 LB 4 OZ) WHOLE FISH (SUCH AS SEA BASS, BREAM OR SNAPPER), SCALED AND CLEANED

60 G (2¼ OZ) CELERY WITH LEAVES

1 SMALL ONION, PEELED

1 GARLIC CLOVE, PEELED

1 SMALL HANDFUL FLAT-LEAF PARSLEY WITH STALKS

130 G (4¾ OZ) MEDIUM-GRAIN RICE

JUICE OF 2 LEMONS

2 EGGS

BEST OLIVE OIL, TO SERVE

This is probably the most well known of Greek soups. It is often made with chicken and sometimes even lamb. Here, the boiled fish is lovely served after the soup, with a drizzle of olive oil or a dish of skordalia (a small scattering of cinnamon over the soup is also lovely).

Cut the head and tail off the fish but don't discard them. Put the celery, onion, garlic, parsley and 2½ litres (87 fl oz/10 cups) of water in a large wide pot. Season with salt and pepper and bring to the boil. Add the fish body, head and tail. Simmer, uncovered, for 20 to 30 minutes, depending on the thickness of the fish. Skim off any scum that may settle on the surface. Remove from the heat. Discard the head and tail and gently take out the fish. Take off the skin and carefully remove the natural long fillets, discarding the spine and bones. Put the fillets on a plate, cover and keep warm. Discard the celery, onion, garlic and parsley and strain the broth into a clean pot. You should have about 1.5 litres (52 fl oz/6 cups). Add the rice and simmer, for about 20 minutes or until tender.

Whisk the lemon juice and eggs with a little salt in a bowl. Add a ladleful of hot broth to acclimatise the egg, then slowly stir the lot back into the broth. Immediately remove from the heat and stir long enough for the egg to just cook through but not form scrambled bits. Taste for salt.

Ladle the soup into bowls and grind a little pepper on top. Serve the fish after or next to the soup, with a drizzle of olive oil.

PSARI VRASTO LADOLEMONO POACHED FISH WITH LEMON OIL

Ψάρι Βραστό (λαδολέμονο)

SERVES 3

1 LARGE POTATO, PEELED, HALVED AND CUT INTO 5 OR 6 PIECES

2 CARROTS, CUT INTO 3 CM (1¼ INCH) ROUNDS

2 ZUCCHINI (COURGETTES), CUT INTO 2–3 CM (¾–1¼ INCH) ROUNDS

1 SMALL CELERY STALK WITH LEAVES (ABOUT 60 G/2¼ OZ), OR SMALL BUNCH OF GREEK-STYLE CELERY

ABOUT 40 G (1½ OZ) ROUND SPRING ONIONS, WHITE PART ONLY

1 FIRM BONELESS WHITE FISH FILLET SUCH AS OCEAN PERCH OR LING (ABOUT 440 G/15½ OZ)

1 TABLESPOON ROUGHLY CHOPPED FLAT-LEAF PARSLEY

LEMON OIL

JUICE OF 1 LARGE JUICY LEMON

4 TABLESPOONS BEST-QUALITY EXTRA VIRGIN OLIVE OIL

I love this. It's delicate yet aromatic, not quite a soup. It is an easy, healthy, almost instant food that you could serve to any generation. You will need a nice big and wide pot here as there is not too much liquid and the ingredients all need to float comfortably. You can use any firm white fish fillets that won't break up too much.

Greek celery is amazing and seems to give a wonderful flavour to their soups. It is lovely clumps and small thin stalks and leaves that look almost like parsley – you might never guess that it's celery if you found it at the market.

Put the potato, carrot, zucchini, celery and onion into a wide pot and add 750 ml (26 fl oz/3 cups) of water. Season with salt. Bring to the boil and simmer uncovered for about 15 minutes. Add the fish, shuffling the vegetables if necessary to ensure that the fish is covered by broth. Simmer, uncovered, over low heat for 10 to 15 minutes (depending on the thickness of the fish) until the fish is cooked through but not breaking up.

For the lemon oil, whip the lemon juice and oil with a little salt in a bowl until thick and creamy. Remove the soup from the heat and discard the onion and celery. Pour in the lemon oil and rock the pot to distribute it well. Leave it for a few minutes so the flavours mingle, and check your seasoning. Scatter in the parsley. Remove the fish to a bowl and break it up into 3 pieces using a fork and spoon. To serve, put 1 piece of fish per bowl, a couple of pieces of each vegetable, a good ladleful of broth and a grind of pepper.

TRAHANA DRIED WHEAT + YOGHURT SOUP

Τραχανάς

SERVES 6

200 G (7 OZ) TRAHANA

1 VEGETABLE STOCK CUBE (NO MSG, FROM HEALTH FOOD SHOPS), OR 2 CUPS HOMEMADE VEGETABLE BROTH

ABOUT 375 ML (13 FL OZ/ 1½ CUPS) MILK

200 G (7 OZ) FETA, CUT INTO LARGE BLOCKS

OLIVE OIL, TO SERVE

LEMON QUARTERS, TO SERVE

Trahana is bulgur (burghul) wheat dried with yoghurt, popular in villages and mountains. It is available from Greek food stores. There are two types, sweet and sour – I love the sour one.

Trahana is wonderful – I have loved it since I was small, but I know friends who used to come to us were a bit surprised by it. It may take some getting used to but it feels like one of those soups you would imagine from a Russian fairy tale. When cooked it becomes a creamy thin savoury porridge. Perfect for a cold winter night. Chunks of feta are added at the end and heated to just surrender stage. The soup is served with a drizzle of olive oil and those who want can squeeze some lemon in, even though the soup itself is a bit on the sour side.

Keep any uncooked trahana in a sealed bag in the fridge.

Put the trahana into a wide pot. Cover with 1 litre (35 fl oz/4 cups) of hot water, put the lid on and leave for about 3 hours. Add the stock cube with another 500 ml (17 fl oz/2 cups) of hot water (or homemade broth), bring to the boil then simmer, uncovered, for about 45 minutes, stirring often so the trahana doesn't catch on the bottom. Halfway through, add the milk and a cup of water. You want it thick but spoonable, so add extra water if necessary to thin it down; you could need quite a bit more or none, depending on your trahana. It should melt to a creamy thin porridge, but if it is very chunky to start with, you might have to pulse with a hand-held blender to get rid of any chunky bits. Add the feta in the last few minutes, just long enough to soften but keep the pieces whole. Serve in bowls with a splash of olive oil, some pepper and a squeeze of lemon.

FASOLADA WHITE BEAN SOUP

Φασολάδα

SERVES 6

500 G (1 LB 2 OZ) DRIED BUTTER (OR CANNELLINI, HARICOT, NAVY) BEANS

3 GARLIC CLOVES, 1 WHOLE, 2 CHOPPED

1 BAY LEAF

1 SMALL CELERY STALK

½ SMALL ONION

4 TABLESPOONS OLIVE OIL

1 LARGE ONION, CHOPPED

3 CARROTS, PEELED, CUT INTO NICE CHUNKS

400 G (14 OZ) TIN CHOPPED TOMATOES

50 G (1¾ OZ) RED OR ROUND SPRING ONIONS, ROUGHLY CHOPPED

½ CUP VERY ROUGHLY CHOPPED FLAT-LEAF PARSLEY

¼ CUP ROUGHLY CHOPPED CELERY LEAVES

BEST OLIVE OIL, TO SERVE

This is a wonderful wintry chunky soup. My friend Lisa brought this version to our table ready cooked one Sunday for lunch, which I love. Depending on the beans you use, you may need to add more water. Often smaller beans are used but this is also lovely with the bigger butter beans. This was originally a poor man's dish. Cheap and filling but beloved and comforting, and people would often exclaim, 'If only we had a fasolada now!' Use best-quality olive oil.

Cover the beans with plenty of cold water and soak overnight. Next day drain and rinse them, and put into a pot with cold water to cover. Bring to the boil, skimming off any scum that has formed. Drain and rinse again. Wipe any scum that has collected on the pot then return the beans to it. Add 2 litres (70 fl oz/ 8 cups) of cold water, the whole garlic clove, bay leaf, celery stalk and the ½ onion. Simmer, partly covered, for about an hour, until tender. Larger beans will take longer and will need more water. Add salt in the last 10 minutes or so.

Meanwhile, heat the oil in a soup pot and sauté the chopped onion (not the spring onion) until soft and golden. Add the chopped garlic and carrots and when the garlic smells good, add the tomatoes. Season with salt and pepper. Swish about 125 ml (70 fl oz/½ cup) of water in the tomato tin and pour into the pot. Put the lid on and simmer for 10 minutes or so. When the beans are ready, pour them and their water in with the tomato sauce. Simmer for 10 minutes, adding a little water if it's too thick. Ladle into bowls and serve with onion, parsley and celery leaves on top, a drizzle of oil and a grind of pepper.

FAKES LENTIL SOUP

Φακές

SERVES 5 OR 6

6 TABLESPOONS RED WINE VINEGAR

4 GARLIC CLOVES, PEELED

1 DRIED OREGANO SPRIG, OR 1 FRESH ROSEMARY SPRIG

2 BAY LEAVES

300 G (10½ OZ) SMALL BROWN LENTILS

6 TABLESPOONS OLIVE OIL

1 LARGE ONION, FINELY CHOPPED

1 CARROT

1 CINNAMON ROLL

300 G (10½ OZ) RIPE TOMATOES, COARSELY GRATED (SO THE SKIN STAYS BEHIND IN YOUR HAND)

BEST OLIVE OIL, FOR SERVING

This is a soup that most Greeks have grown up with. The unusual part of this healthy, nourishing soup is the way they serve it with a drizzle of vinegar. They say that the vitamins in carrots help to absorb the iron in lentils better and so they should be cooked together.

Put the vinegar into a bowl. Squash 1 of the garlic cloves and add it to the bowl along with the oregano or rosemary sprig and 1 of the bay leaves. Leave aside for now.

Rinse the lentils then put them into a pot with 1.75 litres (61 fl oz/ 7 cups) of cold water. Add the remaining garlic cloves and bay leaf, the olive oil, onion, carrot and cinnamon roll and bring to the boil. Skim the surface if necessary, cover and simmer gently for about 25 minutes. Add the tomato, season well with salt and a little pepper and simmer for 20 minutes, or until the lentils are soft and the soup is lovely and thick. Take the lid off and simmer for about 5 minutes or longer if necessary until it has a lovely thick soupy consistency. Take off the heat, splash in 3 tablespoons of the vinegar and leave it to stand for a few minutes before serving.

Serve hot, with an extra drizzle of olive oil and with the remaining vinegar on the table for anyone who'd like more.

LADERA

+SALADS

The smell of a Greek manavi (green grocers) ... especially old-style ones or on the islands re-blossoms each time I walk into one. It is a warm, extremely friendly and comforting smell ... like flowers, leaves, melons, figs, meadows, orchards, the sea and sweet life all rolled into one shop.

REVITHADA BAKED CHICKPEAS

Ρεβυθάδα

SERVES MANY

500 G (1 LB 2 OZ) DRIED
CHICKPEAS

1 TABLESPOON PLAIN
(ALL-PURPOSE) FLOUR

2 ONIONS, WELL CHOPPED

2 BAY LEAVES

6 TABLESPOONS OLIVE OIL

BEST OLIVE OIL, TO SERVE

LEMON QUARTERS,
TO SERVE

The traditional Sunday lunch in Sifnos is chickpeas. The skepastaria, or special ceramic pot, which is often passed down from mother to daughter, is taken on Saturday afternoon to the baker to cook overnight in the wood oven. Then everyone collects theirs on Sunday morning.

Here the chickpeas are cooked for quite a while in a regular oven.

If you have a ceramic pot of about 23 cm (9 inches) in diameter which has a lid, great. If not, a casserole pot will work well. It really is the pot, good olive oil and maybe the wonderful surrounds of a Greek island that can make a dish special.

Put the chickpeas and flour in a bowl, cover with plenty of cold water and soak overnight. Preheat the oven to 200°c (400°f/gas 6). Drain the chickpeas, rinse and put into a large round ceramic pot which has a good-fitting lid. Cover with 1 litre (35 fl oz/4 cups) of water and add the onion, bay leaves and olive oil. Stir a few times to distribute the onion, then put the lid on. Bake in the oven for 2 hours.

Lower the temperature to 180°c (350°f/gas 4) and remove the pot from the oven. The contents should be nice and bubbly. Season well with salt and pepper and mix through. Return the pot, still covered, to the oven for a further 2 hours, when the chickpeas will be lovely and soft and there is a little of the thick liquid left. Turn off the oven and leave the covered pot to cool down for about 1 hour. Taste for salt and pepper then serve warm, with a drizzle of olive oil and a squeeze of lemon juice if you like.

YIGANDES BAKED GIANT BUTTER BEANS

Γίγαντες

SERVES 6 TO 8

500 G (1 LB 2 OZ) DRIED GIANT BUTTER BEANS

1 BAY LEAF

4 GARLIC CLOVES, 2 WHOLE, 2 CHOPPED

125 ML (4 FL OZ/½ CUP) OLIVE OIL

1 LARGE RED ONION, CHOPPED

400 G (14 OZ) TIN CRUSHED TOMATOES

1 TABLESPOON TOMATO PASTE (CONCENTRATED PUREE)

2 HEAPED TABLESPOONS ROUGHLY CHOPPED FLAT-LEAF PARSLEY

4 THYME SPRIGS

In Greece, a lot of pulses are eaten as a main meal, and their long-cooked beans are especially wonderful. If you can't get the giant beans, then cannellini or other small beans will do. The beans will need soaking overnight. I use a ceramic round dish of about 23 cm (9 inches) in diameter with a lid.

Put the beans in a bowl with plenty of cold water and soak overnight. Drain and rinse, then put into a pot and cover well with water. Bring to the boil, skimming off any scum that comes to the surface. Drain and give the beans a shower in a colander. Wipe off any scum from the sides of the pot. Return the beans to the pot, cover with plenty of water and add the bay leaf and 2 whole garlic cloves. Bring to the boil, lower the heat and cook, partly covered, for about 1¼ hours, until the beans are tender. Skim the surface when

necessary. Add salt just towards the end. Preheat the oven to 180°c (350°f/gas 4).

Meanwhile, heat the oil in a flame-proof casserole dish and sauté the onion until golden. Add the chopped garlic and cook until it smells good, then add the tomato and tomato paste and some salt and pepper. Swill the tomato tin with a few tablespoons of water and add to the tomato. Simmer uncovered for a few minutes. Add the parsley and thyme sprigs. Remove from the heat.

When the beans are tender, transfer with a slotted spoon to the casserole. Add enough of the bean cooking water to just cover. Turn through gently. Taste for salt and pepper. Cover and bake for 45 minutes or until beans are creamy and there is some thickened sauce left in the pot. Take the lid off and bake until a bit crusty on top, 15 minutes or so. Cool a little before serving.

FASOLAKIA YACHNI STEWED GREEN BEANS IN TOMATO

Φασολάκια γιαχνί

SERVES 6 OR SO

ABOUT 800 G (1 LB 12 OZ) FLAT GREEN BEANS

5 TABLESPOONS OLIVE OIL

1 RED ONION, CHOPPED

3 GARLIC CLOVES, CHOPPED

400 G (14 OZ) TIN CRUSHED TOMATOES

2 TABLESPOONS ROUGHLY CHOPPED FLAT-LEAF PARSLEY

¼ TEASPOON GROUND CINNAMON

This is often served as a main course in Greece, with feta to mingle in with the sauce, and bread. Of course it's also great served next to a main course such as roast meat, or fish.

I have also seen potatoes added to the stew.

Cut the tops off the green beans and string them if necessary. Rinse and drain, keeping them in your colander for now.

Heat the olive oil in a large non-stick pot and sauté the onion until softened and almost sticky. Add the garlic and, when you can smell it, add the tomato, parsley, 2 or 3 grinds of pepper and a good amount of salt. Simmer, uncovered, over medium heat for about 8 minutes, until the tomatoes soften and collapse.

Add the beans and 250 ml (9 fl oz / 1 cup) of hot water. Scatter the cinnamon over the beans and put the lid on. When it comes to the boil, turn the beans through then put the lid back on and simmer until the beans are soft, about 20 minutes, turning through a few times so that no lonely beans sit out of the sauce for long. At the end of this time there should be a good amount of thickish sauce. If you think it needs it, stir in a little water. Now turn off the heat and leave them for a while, covered, to absorb the flavours. Take the pot to the table and serve warm.

BAMIES BAKED OKRA

Mπάμιες

SERVES 8 OR SO

600 G (1 LB 5 OZ) SMALL OKRA

80 ML (2½ FL OZ/⅓ CUP) WINE VINEGAR

1 TABLESPOON COARSE SALT

6 TABLESPOONS OLIVE OIL

1 LARGE RED ONION, CHOPPED

2 SMALL GREEN SWEET PEPPERS (ABOUT 60 G/ 2¼ OZ EACH), HALVED LENGTHWAYS, SEEDED, SLICED

2 GARLIC CLOVES, FINELY CHOPPED

400 G (14 OZ) TIN CHOPPED TOMATOES

2 TABLESPOONS CHOPPED FLAT-LEAF PARSLEY

Okra are enjoyed in Greece when they are in season. They are often stewed on the stovetop but here they are baked, which I really like. Also called ladies' fingers, they are rather a particular vegetable, containing a glutinous substance which thickens dishes. They are great served with a dish of feta and some bread and perhaps a green salad. Try and get small okra of around 4 cm (1½ inches) in length, so there is less chance of tough or stringy ones. This dish is sometimes also baked with chicken pieces in it.

Rinse and drain the okra. Trim the top of their hard stems in a circular conical way so that the top isn't pierced and no seeds can leak out. Put them into a bowl of cold water with the vinegar and salt and leave for an hour or so. Drain into a colander and rinse well.

Preheat the oven to 180°c (350°f/gas 4). Heat the olive oil in a non-stick frying pan and sauté the onion until soft and sticky. Add the peppers towards the end, sauté for a couple of minutes, then add the garlic. When you can smell it frying, add the tomatoes. Simmer for about 5 minutes, mashing any tomato lumps with a wooden spoon. Stir in 500 ml (17 fl oz/2 cups) of water and the parsley, and season with salt and pepper. Add the okra, gently turning them to coat well.

Turn out into a 22 x 30 cm (8½ x 12 inch) baking dish and bake uncovered for about 50 minutes. Gently turn the okra over and continue baking until the okra are roasted looking and the sauce is thick and dark and no longer watery, about 30 minutes. If it seems like the okra are getting too dark too quickly, turn the oven down slightly. Taste one to see if it is lovely and soft. Cool a little before serving to allow the okra to absorb the juices.

BRIAM MIXED ROAST VEGETABLES

Μπριάμ

SERVES 6 TO 8

2 SMALL EGGPLANTS
(AUBERGINES) (600 G/1 LB
5 OZ TOTAL)

2–3 ZUCCHINI
(COURGETTES) (300 G/
10½ OZ TOTAL), CUT INTO
1.5 CM (⅝ INCH) SLICES

5–6 TOMATOES (800 G/
1 LB 12 OZ TOTAL), HALF
GRATED, HALF CUT INTO
CHUNKS

300 G (10½ OZ) POTATOES,
CUT INTO 1 CM (½ INCH)
SLICES

1 LARGE RED ONION,
CUT INTO THIN RINGS

ABOUT 5 SMALL RED
PEPPERS OR 1 LARGE RED
CAPSICUM (PEPPER), CUT
INTO THICK STRIPS

8 TABLESPOONS OLIVE OIL

1 TEASPOON DRIED
OREGANO

It's wonderful to have a huge dish of mixed roasted vegetables that can be a meal on its own or can stand next to almost anything. This is nice warm or at room temperature. It will need quite a while in the oven and it is a lovely chunky result. You can also add other vegetables of your choice.

Quarter the eggplants lengthways, then cut into 1 cm (½ inch) slices. Put them in a colander, sprinkle with salt and leave to drain away their juices for about 30 minutes. Wipe dry with paper towels. Preheat the oven to 180°c (350°f/gas 4). Put all the vegetables into a 33 cm (13 inch) or so round, or of similar dimension, ovenproof dish and drizzle the oil over. Add salt and pepper, and crumble the oregano over the top with your fingers. Cover tightly with foil and bake for about 2 hours or until all the vegetables are tender. Remove the foil and roast for 40 minutes or so more, until the vegetables are lovely and roasted and the sauce is reduced and a bit sticky. Taste for salt.

HORTA WILD GREENS

Χόρτα

SERVES 4 TO 6

ABOUT 1 KG (2 LB 4 OZ)
WILD GREENS

BEST OLIVE OIL, TO SERVE

RED WINE VINEGAR,
TO SERVE

LEMON QUARTERS,
TO SERVE

_____

You will find wild greens everywhere in Greece. It's a great idea to order them out – most tavernas seem to have them – and if you have them at the start of your meal, you will have this healthy dish going while you wait for the rest. When you buy them at the market for cooking, you will need an industrial amount even for just one family but even so, it is well worth it. Some are slightly bitter but are very healthy. There are some sweeter varieties called vlita, also grabbed in armfuls from the mountainsides and fields. Use any wild greens that you can find when making them at home or a mixture of a few different ones, such as chicory (witlof), dandelion and mustard leaves, and root vegetable tops such as turnip and beetroot can also be mixed in. You can add a few ladlefuls of the cooking water to a soup or boil some pasta and rice in it, or just drink some of the cooking water with a squeeze of lemon in. Delicious and health giving.

To prepare the greens, snap off and discard any thick stalks, otherwise keep the whole leaf if it is young. Rinse them in cold water and shake dry. Bring a large pot of salted water to the boil and add the leaves, pushing them down and turning them over with tongs until they have all wilted. Simmer until the leaves are tender, but not soggy and until the stems are no longer crisp – the cooking time will depend on your greens. Drain well.

To serve, drizzle with olive oil and splash over a little vinegar. Serve some lemon on the side.

ANGINARES ME KOUKIA ARTICHOKES + BROAD BEANS

Αγγινάρες Με Κουκιά

SERVES 8

1.5 KG (3 LB 5 OZ) BROAD (FAVA) BEANS IN THEIR PODS (250 G/9 OZ PODDED AND SKINNED)

JUICE OF 2½ LEMONS

8 ARTICHOKES (220 G/ 7¾ OZ EACH) WITH A STEM OF ABOUT 6 CM (2½ INCHES)

125 ML (4 FL OZ/½ CUP) OLIVE OIL

100 G (3½ OZ, ABOUT 3 LARGE) ROUND SPRING ONIONS, TRIMMED, ROUGHLY CHOPPED

2 TABLESPOONS CHOPPED DILL

1 TABLESPOON ROUGHLY CHOPPED MINT

This is a beautiful spring dish. It can be served as a side dish or as a main with a plate of feta and some bread. Freshly podded peas are also lovely here if you prefer them to the broad beans. Drizzle a little extra olive oil over to serve, and pepper.

Pod the beans and take off their outer jackets (if they don't come off easily you can drop them in boiling water for a few seconds). The small very green beans can be left, as their jackets are not tough. Put the juice of 1½ lemons in a large bowl (non-metallic) of cold water. Snap the tough outer leaves off the artichokes and discard. You may need to remove more than you think before you get to the tender leaves. Slice off the hard top of the leaves, maybe even one-third of the top depending on the size and type of artichoke. Leave 4 cm (1½ inches) or so of stalk and cut off the rest. Using a potato peeler or small sharp knife, peel the stems and the base of the artichokes. Halve them from top to bottom then remove the choke with a small knife or pointed spoon. Put the cleaned artichokes immediately into the lemon water to prevent them from darkening.

Heat the oil in a large non-stick frying pan. Add the onion and gently sauté until pale gold.

Drain the artichokes, pat dry with paper towels and add them to the pan in a single layer. Cook, turning once, until slightly coloured. Season with salt and pepper, add 250 ml (9 fl oz/1 cup) of water, put the lid on and simmer for 10 minutes or until just tender and there is a little thickened sauce left in the pan. If there isn't much sauce left, add a little hot water. Add the broad beans, leave the lid off and cook for another few minutes. Sprinkle in the remaining lemon juice, dill and mint, rocking the pan for everything to mingle. Remove from the heat and leave for a few minutes before serving. This can also be served at room temperature, but is best warm.

The same ingredients are lovely served raw with best olive oil, a piece of cheese and bread, pita or koulouria. Simply shelled broad beans, cleaned artichokes, spring onions, fresh dill and mint leaves. Serve with ouzo on ice.

EHI TIS ORES TOU – IT HAS ITS MOMENTS

said the barman while I was waiting for a freshly squeezed orange juice and the juicer wasn't working. There was a lovely acceptance in this ...

PANTZAROSALATA BEETROOT WITH YOGHURT + PISTACHIOS

Παντζαροσαλάτα

SERVES 4 TO 6

650 G (1 LB 7 OZ) BEETROOT
(ABOUT 4), TRIMMED OR
500 G (1 LB 2 OZ) READY-
COOKED BEETROOT

3 TABLESPOONS OLIVE OIL

JUICE OF ½ LEMON

2 GARLIC CLOVES, FINELY
CHOPPED

3 TABLESPOONS COARSELY
CHOPPED FLAT-LEAF
PARSLEY

340 G (11¾ OZ/1⅓ CUPS)
GREEK YOGHURT

10 G (¼ OZ) SHELLED
PISTACHIO NUTS, CHOPPED

This is the way my friend Annette makes her beetroot salad. I love the colours here. And its freshness, even though it looks mayonnaisy; it's a surprise to remember that it's actually much lighter than it looks.

This is wonderful with fresh, roasted beetroot, or you can also use ready cooked beetroots in which case it will only take a second to put together. If you are using fresh ones and they have leaves you can boil those too for a few minutes and dress them with olive oil to serve.

If using fresh, cut the leaves well above the bulb so that they don't bleed.

Preheat the oven to 180°c (350°f/gas 4). Wash the beetroots well, being careful not to pierce their skins. Cut off the leaves, leaving 2 to 3 cm (1 inch) attached so the beetroot doesn't bleed, and leave the root for now. Wrap each beetroot individually in foil and bake for about 1 hour until tender when tested with a sharp knife.

Whip the oil lightly in a bowl with the lemon juice and garlic.

Wearing kitchen gloves, peel the beetroot. Trim away the root and cut them into nice chunks. If you are using ready-cooked beetroot, rinse if necessary and trim away any tough end bits and cut into chunks. Put in a bowl. Add the lemon oil, parsley and season with salt and pepper. Add the yoghurt and mix all through gently. Scatter the pistachio nuts on top and serve.

SALATA HORIATIKI GREEK SALAD

Χωριάτικη

SERVES 2 TO 4

8 GORGEOUS SMALL RIPE TOMATOES, QUARTERED

1 CUCUMBER (200 G/7 OZ), SLICED THICKLY ON THE DIAGONAL

1 SMALL–MEDIUM RED ONION, SLICED

ABOUT 17 DRAINED KALAMATA OLIVES IN BRINE

1 HEAPED TABLESPOON CAPERS

2 SMALL HANDFULS OF GLISTRIDA (PURSLANE) IF YOU CAN GET IT

150 G (5½ OZ) SLAB OF FETA

1 TEASPOON OR SO DRIED OREGANO

4 TABLESPOONS OLIVE OIL

1 TABLESPOON RED WINE VINEGAR, OPTIONAL

The quality of tomatoes, olive oil and the other ingredients is really important to make the kind of salad at home that one will have eaten on holiday near a sun-soaked beach.

You can add a handful of other greens instead of the glistrida (purslane), if you like, but the padded thickness of their leaves is great, or just leave it plain. Many Greeks use only olive oil to dress their salads, while others add a little red wine vinegar. The juices at the bottom of the bowl are enjoyed and bread is used for 'papara', the soaking of bread in the juices before eating. In some places in Greece they serve a dollop of mizithra cheese on top instead of feta.

Put the tomatoes, cucumber, onion, olives and capers into a serving bowl. Add the glistrida (purslane) and season with a little salt and a few grinds of pepper. Put the feta on top and crumble the oregano over with your fingers. Drizzle the olive oil over, and the vinegar if using. Serve with bread.

SALATA MAROULI LETTUCE SALAD

Σαλάτα μαρούλι

SERVES 6 TO 8

400 G (14 OZ) COS (ROMAINE) LETTUCE

2 TABLESPOONS CHOPPED DILL

40 G (1½ OZ) ROUND SPRING ONION, OR RED ONION, SLICED

4 TABLESPOONS OLIVE OIL

JUICE OF ½ LARGE LEMON

So plain yet so good, and it goes well with many things. One of the plain salads always available in Greece. Use best-quality extra virgin olive oil.

Rinse the lettuce, shake it dry, then shred the leaves. Pat them dry with paper towels. Put in a bowl with the dill and onion. Dress with the olive oil and lemon juice just before eating. Add salt and pepper and toss lightly.

TOMATOSALATA TOMATO SALAD

Ντοματοσαλάτα

SERVES A FEW

6 LOVELY RIPE JUICY TOMATOES (ABOUT 1 KG/ 2 LB 4 OZ)

100 G (3½ OZ) KALAMATA OLIVES

2 TABLESPOONS CAPERS

4 TABLESPOONS OLIVE OIL

1 TEASPOON DRIED OREGANO

In Greece a whole big beautiful tomato could make a meal as it's so good on its own, just with a little salt and olive oil. A salad like this works well next to grilled foods such as bifteki.

Cut the tomatoes into nice chunks. Put them into a bowl with the olives, capers and olive oil, and season to taste with salt and pepper. Crumble the oregano over. Toss gently, and serve.

PATATOSALATA
POTATO SALAD

Πατατοσαλάτα

SERVES 4 TO 6

800 G (1 LB 12 OZ) WASHED UNPEELED POTATOES

4 ANCHOVY FILLETS, ROUGHLY CHOPPED

40 G (1½ OZ) KALAMATA OLIVES

2 TABLESPOONS CAPERS

2–3 TRIMMED ROUND SPRING ONIONS (80 G/ 2¾ OZ) INCLUDING SOME GREEN PARTS, SLICED

4 HEAPED TABLESPOONS ROUGHLY CHOPPED FLAT-LEAF PARSLEY

ABOUT 6 TABLESPOONS OLIVE OIL

ABOUT 2 TABLESPOONS RED WINE VINEGAR

This goes very well with all grilled fish dishes. You could also add a couple of boiled eggs in here. Use lemon juice instead of the vinegar if you prefer.

Boil the potatoes in salted water until tender but not too soft. Drain, and leave to cool for 10 minutes or so before pulling the skins away. Cut up into good chunks and put into a serving bowl. Add the anchovy, olives, capers, onion, parsley, olive oil and vinegar, and season with pepper. Toss through gently, trying not to break up the potatoes. Taste for salt and serve warm, or at room temperature. Even nice served cold the next day.

SALATA POLITIKI CABBAGE + PEPPER SALAD

Σαλάτα πολίτικη

SERVES MANY, MANY

1 SMALL CABBAGE (1.2 KG/ 2 LB 10 OZ)

400 G (14 OZ) CARROTS, COARSELY GRATED

400 G (14 OZ) SMALL GREEN SWEET PEPPERS, SLICED

400 G (14 OZ) SMALL RED SWEET PEPPERS, SLICED

50 G (1¾ OZ) GREEK CELERY (OR THIN YOUNG STALKS WITH SOME LEAVES), CHOPPED

180 ML (6 FL OZ) RED WINE VINEGAR

3 TABLESPOONS SALT

3 GARLIC CLOVES, CHOPPED

GENEROUS PINCH OF CRUSHED GROUND CHILLIES

OLIVE OIL, TO SERVE

LEMON QUARTERS, TO SERVE

If this amount seems crazy, then just make half a portion. It's a lovely huge amount to make and it keeps well in the fridge, covered for 5 to 6 days after it has been made. It will need a few days first in the fridge to drag out the juices before you can eat it. The red and green peppers used for this are the small, long and thin Greek ones.

Discard the outer leaves of the cabbage. Halve and core it, then shred medium-fine. Put in a large bowl with everything else except the olive oil and lemons. Roll up your sleeves and mix and knead everything together well with your hands. It needs a lot of pressing about. Cover and leave in the fridge for 3 days before tasting. But in the meantime turn it through each day to drag all the juices out.

Serve the salad drizzled with olive oil and a squeeze of lemon juice if you like.

ΤΙΜΟΛΟΓΙΟΝ

	δρχ
ΚΑΦΕΣ	0.6
ΚΑΚΑΟ	0.6
ΤΕΪΟΝ	0.6
ΓΛΥΚΑ κουτ.	0.60
ΛΕΜΟΝΑΔΑ	0.60
ΠΟΡΤΟΚΑΛ.	0.60
ΚΟΚΑ-ΚΟΛΑ	0.60
ΠΕΨΙ-ΚΟΛΑ	0.6
ΟΥΖΟ γαρ.	
ΜΠΥΡΑ	0.9
ΚΡΑΣΙ	1
ΣΟΔΑ	0.

Γ. ΟΙΚΟΝΟΜΟΥ

MAYIREFTA

READY-COOKED FOODS

There are some restaurants in Greece that only serve mayirefta (cooked) foods, and these will be all the dishes that need a long time in the oven and can't be prepared then and there to order. The Greek tapsi is something wonderful. Something vital. Tapsi is a roasting dish, often used to refer to a quantity – 1 tapsi of this or that – and it has a wonderful connotation in Greece. There is something very encouraging about large tapsis, and large families everywhere.

PSARI FOURNOU ALA SPETSIOTA BAKED FISH WITH TOMATO

Ψάρι α λα σπετσιώτα

SERVES 4

4 X 200 G (7 OZ) OR SO THICK, FIRM, SKINLESS WHITE FISH FILLETS

3 TABLESPOONS OLIVE OIL

JUICE OF 2 LEMONS

60 ML (2 FL OZ/¼ CUP) WHITE WINE

3 GARLIC CLOVES, CHOPPED

400 G (14 OZ) TIN CHOPPED TOMATOES

40 G (1½ OZ) CELERY STALK WITH LEAVES, CHOPPED

4 HEAPED TABLESPOONS CHOPPED FLAT-LEAF PARSLEY

OLIVE OIL, TO SERVE

Bass, snapper, grouper, kingclip or perch are good here. This is so simple to prepare you will hardly believe it. You will need an oven dish that will hold the fish fillets in a single layer – so of course with a bigger dish you can up the ingredients. This is nice served with boiled potatoes, also showered with chopped parsley and a drizzle of olive oil. Use celery tops with many of the leaves rather than sticks. You might like to add a little chopped chilli into the sauce as well.

Preheat the oven to 180°c (350°f/gas 4). Season the fish fillets with a little salt. In a jug mix the olive oil, lemon juice, wine, garlic, tomato, celery and 3 tablespoons of the parsley. Season with salt and pepper. Splatter a few tablespoons over the bottom of an ovenproof dish large enough to take the fillets comfortably in a single layer. Lie the fish fillets on top and pour over the rest of the tomato mixture. Bake, uncovered, for 45 to 55 minutes, depending on your fish. The sauce should be reduced and the tomato chunks starting to caramelise on the top. If the sauce is still watery, turn the oven off and prop the door open for 10 minutes. Drizzle with a little olive oil, scatter with the remaining parsley and serve with bread.

ARNI YUVETSI BAKED LAMB WITH RICE-SHAPED PASTA

Αρνί γιουβέτσι

SERVES 6

1.3–1.5 KG (3 LB–3 LB 5 OZ) LEG OF LAMB

½ LEMON

125 ML (4 FL OZ/½ CUP) OLIVE OIL

1 TEASPOON SWEET PAPRIKA

2 GARLIC CLOVES, FINELY CHOPPED

150 G (5½ OZ) ROUND SPRING ONIONS (ABOUT 4), QUARTERED AND ROUGHLY CHOPPED

400 G (14 OZ) TIN CRUSHED TOMATOES

½ TEASPOON DRIED OREGANO

1 CINNAMON ROLL

250 G (9 OZ) KRITHARAKI (ALMOND-SHAPED DRIED PASTA)

GRATED KEFALOTIRI OR FIRM MIZITHRA TO SERVE

Yuvetsi is traditionally a Sunday dish. People would put all their ingredients into the 'yuvetsi' (the large ceramic dish that this recipe is cooked in) and take it to the bakers with the packet of kritharaki pasta. You could give any specific instructions to the baker, and he would add the pasta in at the end. Discussions would always be that the baker had done well that time, or perhaps it had got a bit too overcooked – but always it was good. And it would always smell like a whole tavern, having caught all the other interesting smells like roasting chickens in the air. This was a good way for the housewife to rest on a Sunday, and one of the family members, such as her husband or son, would go and collect the yuvetsi. If you don't have a yuvetsi, you can use a good wide, round or rectangular dish and if you can't get the small almond-shaped pasta, you can use another type. This dish is often also made with beef, chicken or octopus. Sometimes the pasta is cooked with no meat, just tomato and coarsely grated firm mizithra.

Preheat the oven to 180°c (350°f/gas 4). Trim any excess fat off the lamb. Squeeze the lemon juice over and massage it in. Put 4 tablespoons of the olive oil in a large (about 36 cm/14¼ inch diameter) baking dish (or a yuvetsi, of course, if you have one). Add the lamb, then drizzle the rest of the oil over it. Rub the paprika and garlic onto the lamb and season well with salt and pepper. Add the onion, tomato, oregano and cinnamon to the dish and sprinkle with some salt too. Put in the oven and roast for 30 minutes. Add 250 ml (9 fl oz/1 cup) of hot

continued

water and cook for an hour, turning the lamb halfway through.

In the meantime, boil the pasta in lightly salted water until just done. Drain. When the lamb is done, add the pasta around it in the dish with 375 ml (13 fl oz/1½ cups) of hot water and gently mix into the tomato, trying not to get the pasta on the lamb. Return to the oven for 10 or 15 minutes, or until the pasta has absorbed quite a bit of the liquid but is still nice and saucy. Remove from the oven and rest in a warm spot for 5 minutes. Grind a little pepper over and take the whole dish to the table for serving, with the cheese on the side for whoever wants.

ARNI MASTELO LAMB IN A FLOWER POT WITH DILL + RED WINE

Αρνι μαστέλο

SERVES 6

A FEW DRY GRAPEVINE BRANCHES

A LARGE HANDFUL OF DILL, STALKS AND LEAVES TOGETHER

2 SHOULDERS OF LAMB (ABOUT 1.7 KG/3 LB 12 OZ TOTAL WITH BONE), CUT INTO LARGE CHUNKS BY YOUR BUTCHER

2 TABLESPOONS OLIVE OIL

500 ML (17 FL OZ/2 CUPS) RED WINE

A NICE HANDFUL OF CHOPPED DILL, FOR SERVING

I love this for its simplicity. And for the very fact that it's cooked in a flower pot (with no hole in the bottom!). On Sifnos, the lamb is slowly cooked with red wine, flavoured with dill or fennel, over dried vines in a clay 'mastelo' or pot. A few vine branches are arranged in a criss-cross pattern to form a grid on the base of the pot. This adds flavour to the lamb and makes it tender. You can use an ordinary ceramic dish if you don't have a suitable flower pot. Preferably with a lid and roughly 24 cm (9½ inches) will do.

Preheat the oven to 200°c (400°f/gas 6). Arrange 2 or 3 vine branches (breaking them up if necessary) over the bottom of a wide terracotta pot of about 24 cm (9½ inches) diameter and 10 cm (4 inches) high, if yours is much wider, you may need to add a bit more wine. Put some of the dill in too. Rinse the lamb or wipe the pieces all over with a damp cloth. Lay them on top of the branches, layering the dill and salting and peppering as you go. Drizzle in the oil and pour in the wine. Cover with a lid or several layers of foil and bake for 2 to 2½ hours, turning the lamb and basting a couple of times. The lamb should be melting soft and there will be quite a bit of sauce. If you are not serving immediately, turn the oven off and leave the pot in, still covered, while it cools down.

Serve with a little of the sauce dribbled over and scattered with the chopped dill. Nice with soft roasted or boiled potatoes.

ARNI FRICASSÉE LAMB WITH LETTUCE

Αρνί φρικασέ

SERVES 4

2 COS (ROMAINE) LETTUCES
(ABOUT 700 G/1 LB 9 OZ
TOTAL)

4 LARGE ROUND SPRING
ONIONS (ABOUT 220 G/7¾ OZ
TOTAL)

1.35 KG (3 LB) SHOULDER
OF LAMB WITH BONE, CUT
INTO LARGE EVEN CHUNKS,
(ROUGHLY 5–6 CM/2–2½
INCHES) BY YOUR BUTCHER

8 TABLESPOONS OLIVE OIL

3 GARLIC CLOVES,
2 CHOPPED, 1 WHOLE

185 ML (6 FL OZ/¾ CUP)
WHITE WINE

375 ML (13 FL OZ/1½ CUPS)
HOT VEGETABLE STOCK,
MADE WITH AN MSG-FREE
CUBE, OR HOMEMADE

1 SMALL CELERY STALK
(60 G/2¼ OZ), WELL
CHOPPED

A PINCH OF GROUND CHILLI

2 EGGS

JUICE OF 2 LEMONS

1 HEAPED TABLESPOON
ROUGHLY CHOPPED DILL

1 TABLESPOON ROUGHLY
CHOPPED MINT

The lettuce in this dish is often added to the pot and it's all cooked on the stove top. Here the lamb is baked and the lettuce is softened separately in a pan but the flavours all unite, nevertheless, on the plate.

The dish is finished with an egg and lemon sauce, very typical in Greece.

Preheat the oven to 180°c (350°f/gas 4). Trim away the core of the lettuces and separate the leaves. Rinse and drain them, and shake off any excess water. Cut across the leaves into 3 to 4 cm (1¼ to 1½ inch) strips and keep in a colander for now. Trim away the thick outer layer from the onions, but leave the green stems on. Quarter them lengthways so you have nice long pieces. Rinse and drain. Trim the lamb of any excess fat but you can leave some of the nicer looking fat on. Rinse and pat the pieces dry with paper towels, making sure that there are no stray shards of bone.

Drizzle 5 tablespoons of the oil into a flame-proof non-stick roasting dish of about 30 x 22 cm (12 x 8½ inches). Add the lamb, toss to coat with the oil and roast for 30 minutes. Turn the lamb over and roast for another 30 minutes. Add the spring onion, chopped garlic, wine, and salt and pepper to taste. Roast for a further 30 minutes, or until the lamb is browned and tender. Keep an eye on the onion and the garlic that they are not burning. Add the stock and cook for 10 minutes or so.

Meanwhile, heat the remaining oil in a large non-stick frying pan. Add the whole garlic clove, celery and chilli and sauté until the celery is softened and golden. Add the lettuce, squashing it all in. Sprinkle with salt and pepper, cover, and simmer for 10 to 12 minutes or until the lettuce has wilted and all the liquid has evaporated. Keep hot.

Whip the eggs in a bowl then beat the lemon juice in. Sprinkle a little salt in. Remove the roasting dish from the oven and transfer the lamb and onion to a plate. Pour a cup of the hot liquid from the dish into the egg and lemon juice mixture, beating well to acclimatise. Pour back into the roasting dish and put over the lowest possible flame, stirring and mixing constantly with a wooden spoon until the sauce thickens a little and has a creamy consistency. Remove from the heat. Return the lamb to the dish and shuffle the pieces about to coat with the sauce. Make sure that the lettuce is hot, reheating if necessary. Stir in the dill and mint. Serve some lettuce on each plate with a couple of pieces of lamb and a drizzle of sauce over the top. Grind over some pepper and serve hot.

ISN'T IT LOVELY HOW OUZO CHANGES from transparent to white when water or ice is added?

PATATES FOURNOU ME TOMATES ROAST TOMATO POTATOES

Πατάτες φούρνου με ντομάτες

1.2 KG (2 LB 10 OZ)
POTATOES, PEELED AND
RINSED

2 RIPE TOMATOES,
CUT INTO CHUNKS

1 RED ONION, SLICED

6 TABLESPOONS OLIVE OIL

1 HEAPED TEASPOON
DRIED OREGANO

Preheat the oven to 180°c (350°f/ gas 4). Halve the potatoes lengthways then cut each half into 2 or 3 gondolas, depending on the size of your potatoes. Spread them in a 22 x 30 cm (8½ x 12 inches) non-stick ovenproof dish. Scatter the tomato and onion over, drizzle with the olive oil, and salt and black pepper generously. Crush the oregano between your fingers, letting it fall over the potatoes. Turn the potatoes to coat them well with everything. Dribble 500 ml (17 fl oz/2 cups) of water down the sides of the dish and shuffle it. Roast until the potatoes are tender and melting and the sauce is thick, about 1½ hours. Turn and baste the potatoes every 20 minutes or so and make sure that nothing is sticking to the bottom of the dish and no potatoes are out of the liquid too long and looking plasticy. Taste to see if it needs any salt and pepper. Serve hot.

PATATES FOURNOU LEMONATES ROAST LEMON POTATOES

Πατάτες φούρνου λεμονάτες

SERVES 6

1.2 KG (2 LB/10 OZ) POTATOES, PEELED AND RINSED

JUICE OF 1 LARGE LEMON

6 TABLESPOONS OLIVE OIL

1 HEAPED TEASPOON DRIED OREGANO

These are good with grilled foods. They are not crusty like regular roast potatoes, but soft and moist. You can add more lemon here depending on what you will be serving them with. I use a non-stick oven dish of about 22 x 30 cm (8½ x 12 inches).

Preheat the oven to 180°c (350°f/gas 4). Halve the potatoes lengthways then cut each half into 2 or 3 gondolas, depending on the size of your potatoes. Spread them in a 22 x 30 cm (8½ x 12 inch) non-stick ovenproof dish. Splash the lemon juice and olive oil over them, and salt and pepper generously. Crush the oregano between your fingers, letting it fall over the potatoes. Turn the potatoes to coat them well with everything. Dribble 500 ml (17 fl oz/2 cups) of water down the sides of the dish and give it a shuffle.

Roast until the potatoes are tender and melting and a bit golden here and there with still a bit of sauce in the dish, about 1½ hours, turning and basting them every 20 minutes or so. Add more salt and pepper to taste and serve hot.

KOUNELI STIFADO RABBIT + ONION STEW

Κουνέλι στιφάδο

SERVES 4 TO 6

1 RABBIT (ABOUT 1.25 KG/
2 LB 12 OZ), CLEANED, HEAD
REMOVED

1 KG (2 LB 4 OZ) SMALL
BEAUTIFUL RED ONIONS OR
SHALLOTS (ABOUT 30 G/1 OZ
EACH)

200 ML (7 FL OZ/10
TABLESPOONS) OLIVE OIL

3 TABLESPOONS RED WINE
VINEGAR

250 ML (9 FL OZ/1 CUP)
RED WINE

400 G (14 OZ) TIN CRUSHED
TOMATOES

2 BAY LEAVES

5 ALLSPICE BERRIES

1 CINNAMON ROLL

This is often made with hare which would need longer cooking time, and it is also wonderful with beef or octopus. It's nice and wintry and oniony and goes very well with just a dish of cooked wild greens.

Cut up the rabbit into about 12 pieces. Rinse, and pat dry well with paper towels.

Peel the onions very carefully – the tops and bottoms must remain intact to keep them whole when cooked. Rinse and drain, keeping them in a colander for now.

Preheat the oven to 180°c (350°f/gas 4). Heat 4 tablespoons of the oil in a large non-stick frying pan. Add the pieces of rabbit and fry until nicely golden on all sides. Add the vinegar, season with salt and pepper and cook until reduced to a syrup. Add the wine and simmer for a few minutes before removing the pan from the heat.

Pour the remaining olive oil into a roasting dish of about 33 cm (13 inches) diameter, or a large rectangular one. Tip the rabbit and all the sauce from the pan into the dish, arranging the rabbit over the bottom. Fill in any gaps between the pieces with the onions, then put the rest of the onions on top. Sprinkle some salt and pepper over these. Add the tomato, bay leaves, allspice and cinnamon, and 250 ml (9 fl oz/ 1 cup) of water. Bake, covered with foil, for 1 hour, checking once or twice that nothing is sticking. To loosen things, hold the edges of the dish with oven gloves and give it a good shuffle.

After an hour, shuffle the dish again and turn the onions over, covering them with some of the liquid. Lower the temperature to 160°c (315°f/gas 2–3) and bake for a further 50 minutes, checking and shuffling once or twice. The rabbit should be meltingly tender and the onions soft. Baste everything well. Turn the oven up to 200°c (400°f/gas 6), remove the foil and roast for 10 minutes more to get a bit golden. Serve warm.

VREHI PAPADES KE KAREKLO-PODARA / IT'S RAINING PRIESTS AND CHAIR LEGS

It was raining priests and chair legs in Mani (even though the atmosphere didn't need enhancing). We lunched on tomatoes and almost turquoise olive oil that must have been reflecting the Greek blues, and the onions were as sweet as peaches.

KOTOPOULO FOURNOU ROAST CHICKEN

Κοτόπουλο φούρνου

1.5 KG (3 LB 5 OZ) CHICKEN

1 KG (2 LB 4 OZ) POTATOES (ABOUT 6 MEDIUM), PEELED, HALVED LENGTHWAYS THEN HALVED OR QUARTERED AGAIN INTO GONDOLAS

3 GARLIC CLOVES, PEELED

2 BAY LEAVES

JUICE OF 2 JUICY LEMONS

3 TEASPOONS DRIED OREGANO

6 TABLESPOONS OLIVE OIL

This is a basic, classic type of dish that you would find in many Greek homes. Simple to put together, rustic and very homemadey – left in the oven for a long while to get soft and gooey. You can use a large rectangular non-stick oven dish or a round one.

Preheat the oven to 160°c (315°f/gas 2–3). Rinse the chicken and pat dry well with paper towels. Put breast down into a large roasting dish and scatter the potatoes around with the garlic cloves and bay leaves. Drizzle some lemon juice over the potatoes and inside the chicken, and rub the rest into the skin. Scatter salt and pepper and crumble some of the oregano into the chicken's cavity then rub more salt and pepper and the rest of the oregano over the skin. Drizzle the oil over. Gently pour 250 ml (9 fl oz/ 1 cup) of water around the edges. Roast, basting regularly, for 1½ hours. Now turn the chicken, breast side up, baste again and add 60 ml (2 fl oz/¼ cup) of water. Return to the oven for 1 hour, basting a couple more times and turning the potatoes at least once so they don't dry out. Add 60 ml (2 fl oz/¼ cup) of water 10 or 15 minutes from the end. The chicken should be moist, tender and have a crisp skin, while the potatoes should be moist and soft, not crisp. Rest the chicken for 5 minutes or so before cutting into servings.

KOKKORAS KRASSATOS WINED ROOSTER

Κόκορας κρασάτος

SERVES 4 TO 6

5 TABLESPOONS OLIVE OIL

1 ROOSTER WITH SKIN ON (ABOUT 2.25 KG/5 LB), CUT INTO 10 PIECES

2 RED ONIONS, CHOPPED

3 GARLIC CLOVES, CHOPPED

500 ML (17 FL OZ/2 CUPS) RED WINE

1 HEAPED TABLESPOON TOMATO PASTE (CONCENTRATED PURÉE)

400 G (14 OZ) TIN CHOPPED TOMATOES

½ CINNAMON ROLL

2 BAY LEAVES

3 ALLSPICE BERRIES

HILOPITES (PAGE 248), OR 400 G (14 OZ) DRIED FLAT PASTA PIECES, TO SERVE

GRATED FIRM MIZITHRA, OR HARD SALTED RICOTTA, TO SERVE

This is a dish you may find in villages of Greece. Quite wintry really. It is lovely with homemade noodles (or bought dried ones). It is also often served with chips instead of noodles.

You can use a chicken here in place of the rooster, but the cooking time will be shorter.

Heat the olive oil in a large non-stick pan with high sides and fry the rooster pieces until golden on all sides. Add the onion around the rooster and fry, stirring often, until it is golden, then add the garlic. Season well with salt and pepper on both sides. When it smells good, add the wine.

Simmer uncovered and when much of the wine has evaporated, add the tomato paste, the tomato and a tomato tin of water. Add the cinnamon, bay leaves and allspice, and a little more salt. Bring up to the boil, cover, then reduce the heat to low and simmer for about 2 hours or until the bird is very tender but not falling off the bone. Add a little more water towards the end if the sauce needs loosening up – there must be some nice thickened sauce to serve with the noodles. Turn off the heat and leave, covered.

Cook the hilopites in boiling salted water until soft, a couple of minutes, or follow the packet instructions. Drain and toss with a little of the sauce. Serve straight away, with pieces of rooster on top of the pasta, a little more sauce over and a scattering of cheese.

HILOPITES HOMEMADE NOODLES

Χυλοπίτες

SERVES 4

300 G (10½ OZ/2 CUPS) PLAIN (ALL-PURPOSE) FLOUR

½ TEASPOON SALT

2 EGGS, LIGHTLY BEATEN

1 TABLESPOON OLIVE OIL

3–4 TABLESPOONS MILK

Here is a version if you decide to make your own noodles/pasta. See the egg-free, milk-free version on page 81 suitable for fasting.

These vary in shape – sometimes square and sometimes longer rectangles. The pasta is often well cooked and there is something wonderfully Greek about this.

Put the flour, salt, egg, olive oil and 3 tablespoons of the milk in a bowl and mix well. Knead with lightly floured hands to a firm, smooth dough, adding a little more flour or milk as needed. Wrap in a cloth and leave it for at least half an hour at room temperature.

Divide the dough into quarters.

Keeping the others covered, roll one out as thinly as possible, until almost see-through. You might need to rest and relax it every so often, before continuing to roll some more. Leave each sheet of dough out on the counter while you roll the rest. Starting with the first rolled sheet, cut it into 1.5 cm (⅝ inch) strips, and then into rough rectangles. Leave them out on a lightly floured tray while you cut all the sheets. They can be cooked straight away or left to partially dry, and they can be totally dried but may become fragile.

Put into a large pot of boiling salted water and cook until tender, a couple of minutes. Drain and serve.

YUVARLAKIA DILLED MEATBALLS

Γιουβαρλάκια

SERVES 5 TO 6

400 G (14 OZ) MINCED BEEF

400 G (14 OZ) MINCED PORK

1 EGG, LIGHTLY BEATEN

100 G (3½ OZ) MEDIUM-GRAIN RICE

½ TEASPOON GROUND ALLSPICE

4 VERY HEAPED TABLESPOONS ROUGHLY CHOPPED DILL

4 VERY HEAPED TABLESPOONS ROUGHLY CHOPPED FLAT-LEAF PARSLEY

1 LARGE RED ONION, GRATED ON THE LARGE HOLES OF A GRATER

2 TABLESPOONS OLIVE OIL

160 ML (5¼ FL OZ) MILK

3 TABLESPOONS EACH OF CHOPPED DILL AND PARSLEY STALKS

100 G (3½ OZ) SHELLED PEAS (ABOUT 300 G/10½ OZ UNSHELLED)

2 TABLESPOONS CHOPPED FLAT-LEAF PARSLEY, EXTRA

1 TABLESPOON CHOPPED DILL, EXTRA

2 EGGS

JUICE OF 2 LEMONS

This is a lovely dilly brothy dish to be eaten with a spoon. I use a large cast-iron pot but a high-sided non-stick pan is good too. I love this with some peas, but the traditional way is without.

Mix the minces, egg, rice, allspice, dill, parsley, onion, olive oil and milk in a nice big bowl and add pepper and 1 flat teaspoon of salt. Knead very well. Break off pieces of about 40 g (1½ oz), and roll them into compact balls.

Heat your pot and add the meatballs in 2 batches with no oil. Put the lid on and cook on high heat until the colour of the meatballs changes and they firm up enough for you to turn them. When their undersides are lightly golden, turn them. Cook until golden all over, then remove to a plate. Do the next batch, add all back to the pot and cook until golden. Add 1.5 litres (52 fl oz/6 cups) water, about ½ teaspoon of salt and a little pepper, and the dill and parsley stalks. Cover and simmer gently for about 50 minutes. The meatballs will look like hedgehogs and that's the way they are, but if you boil them too hard, they might break up. Add the peas and simmer until tender but still green, about 10 minutes, it must be nice and brothy (you will still be adding the egg and lemon sauce), add a little more hot water as you think necessary. Add the parsley and dill, then turn off the heat.

Whisk the eggs and lemon juice in a bowl with ½ teaspoon of salt. Add a ladleful of the meatball broth, whisk in to acclimatise, then add another ladleful. Pour it back into the pot and gently stir with a wooden spoon. Leave for a minute or two for the sauce to thicken a bit, holding the pot and shuffling. Taste for salt. Serve warm, with a good grind of pepper.

SOUTZOUKAKIA CUMIN MEATBALLS IN TOMATO

Σουτζουκάκια

SERVES 4 TO 6

100 G (3½ OZ) CRUSTLESS BREAD (ABOUT 3 SLICES), TORN UP

185 ML (6 FL OZ/¾ CUP) MILK

700 G (1 LB 9 OZ) MINCED BEEF

1 EGG, LIGHTLY BEATEN

2 TEASPOONS GROUND CUMIN

2 TABLESPOONS CHOPPED FLAT-LEAF PARSLEY

3 GARLIC CLOVES, 2 FINELY CHOPPED, 1 WHOLE

7 TABLESPOONS OLIVE OIL

2 X 400 G (14 OZ) TINS CRUSHED TOMATOES

125 ML (4 FL OZ/½ CUP) RED WINE

This is often served with rice, mashed potatoes or even chips – which is how I love it. It is a dish that came from Smyrni in Asia Minor when it was part of Greece (now Izmir, Turkey).

The cumin is fabulous in here. If possible try and grind the cumin seeds in a spice grinder.

Put the bread into a bowl, cover with the milk and leave it for about 10 minutes to soak and soften.

In another bowl put the mince, egg, cumin, parsley, chopped garlic, and season with salt and pepper. Squeeze out excess milk from the bread and add the bread to the minced-beef bowl. Mix in very well with a wooden spoon and then with your hands. Form into elongated meatballs of about 50 g (1¾ oz) each. Line them up on a tray and put to one side.

Heat 3 tablespoons of the olive oil in a non-stick pot, add the whole clove of garlic and when that begins to smell good, add the tomato. Season with salt and a little pepper, put the lid on and simmer for 10 minutes or so, squashing out any big lumpy tomato pieces. Heat the remaining olive oil in a large non-stick frying pan that has a lid. Add the soutzoukakia – they should all just fit if you have a big pan. Cook until golden all over, gently turning them with tongs, or by flicking the pan sharply from your wrist if you can manage. When they are nice and gently browned, add the wine and cook for 5 or 6 minutes on high heat until it reduces. Scrape the tomato sauce over the meatballs and bring it to a gentle boil. Lower the heat slightly, put the lid on and simmer for about 20 minutes. Shuffle the pan once or twice to make sure nothing is sticking. There should be a good amount of sauce at the end. Remove from the heat. Leave with the lid on for a few minutes or so before serving.

POLI VARI KE OHI – STRONG BUT NOT

For example ... when you order a Greek coffee, or someone could be 'Poli omorfi ke ohi' beautiful but not. One understands exactly what one means.

PASTITSIO MINCE, MACARONI + BÉCHAMEL LAYERS

Παστίτσιο

SERVES 9 TO 12

400 G (14 OZ) LONG THIN MACARONI

40 G (1½ OZ) GRATED MIZITHRA OR SALTED RICOTTA

MEAT SAUCE

5 TABLESPOONS OLIVE OIL

2 BIG RED ONIONS, GRATED ON THE LARGE HOLES OF A GRATER

800 G (1 LB 12 OZ) BEEF MINCE

200 G (7 OZ) PORK MINCE

2 GARLIC CLOVES, CHOPPED

3 WHOLE CLOVES

3 ALLSPICE BERRIES

250 ML (9 FL OZ/1 CUP) RED WINE

400 G (14 OZ) TIN CHOPPED TOMATOES

1 TABLESPOON TOMATO PASTE (CONCENTRATED PUREE)

2 TABLESPOONS CHOPPED FLAT-LEAF PARSLEY

This large tapsi (dish) should give you leftovers for the next day. It can even be made the day before and heated to serve.

The macaroni mainly used in Greece is about 25 cm (10 inches) long, with a diameter of about 4 mm (⅛ inch) and a hole down the middle. Use something similar if you can't get this exact one.

This is Roulla's pastitsio. She is a lovely lady, and great cook, in Mani. Nikos' mother and Emily's mother-in-law. Roulla said she cooks the whole packet of macaroni anyway, and then she scoops out the extra 100 g (3½ oz) or so and gives it to her husband with some grated mizithra. Probably she's not hungry after tasting her mince and all the rest of her preparations.

For the meat sauce, heat the oil in a large non-stick frying pan that has a lid. Add the onion and both minces and fry over a high heat until all the moisture goes. Add the garlic, cloves and allspice and when that smells good, add the wine. Cook until most of it has evaporated then add the tomato, tomato paste and parsley, and season well with salt and pepper. Stir in 500 ml (17 fl oz/ 2 cups) of hot water. Put the lid on, lower the heat and simmer for about 45 minutes. You want a compact, almost dry sauce so take the lid off for the last 10 minutes if you need to reduce it. Taste for seasoning, put the lid back on and keep aside.

Cook the macaroni in boiling salted water to just done. Drain well by shaking the colander and pressing on the pasta, and if necessary use paper towels to pat up any water that's left. Put into the bottom of a 26 x 34 cm (10½ x 13½ inch) ovenproof dish which is at least 7 cm (2¾ inches) high. Add the grated mizithra, mixing it through the macaroni. Press the pasta down firmly because it needs to be as compact as possible for slicing later.

Preheat the oven to 180°c. (350°f/gas 4). For the béchamel, heat the milk, cinnamon and cloves in a large saucepan. Melt the butter in a large wide pot. Add the flour and stir with a wooden spoon on low heat until smooth, then add warm milk bit by bit, stirring all the time. Now whisk, and when you have a lump-free thick cream, remove from the heat. It's important that it is thick and gloopy on the surface. Break the eggs into a bowl and whisk well. Whisk a ladleful of béchamel into the eggs to acclimatise them, then whisk the whole lot back into the sauce. Add the grated cheese and taste for salt and pepper. Scrape the meat sauce over the pasta in a good level layer and press it down firmly. Pour the béchamel over the top. Bake for 30 to 40 minutes or until the béchamel is firm and golden brown on top. Remove from the oven and allow to cool for about 45 minutes before serving, so that the layers become firm enough to slice. If you try to serve it earlier, it may not hold its shape and may ooze. This is great next day also.

BÉCHAMEL

2 LITRES (70 FL OZ/8 CUPS) MILK

½ TEASPOON GROUND CINNAMON

¼ TEASPOON GROUND CLOVES

240 G (8¾ OZ) UNSALTED BUTTER

250 G (9 OZ/1²/₃ CUPS) PLAIN (ALL-PURPOSE) FLOUR

3 EGGS

80 G (2¾ OZ) COARSELY GRATED MIZITHRA OR SALTED RICOTTA

MOUSSAKA

Μουσακάς

1 KG (2 LB 4 OZ) EGGPLANTS (AUBERGINES)

650 G (1 LB 7 OZ) ZUCCHINI (COURGETTES)

LIGHT OLIVE OIL, FOR FRYING

MEAT SAUCE

5 TABLESPOONS OLIVE OIL

800 G (1 LB 12 OZ) MINCED BEEF

200 G (7 OZ) MINCED PORK

2 BIG RED ONIONS, GRATED ON THE LARGE HOLES OF A GRATER

2 GARLIC CLOVES, CHOPPED

3 WHOLE CLOVES

3 ALLSPICE BERRIES

250 ML (9 FL OZ/1 CUP) RED WINE

400 G (14 OZ) TIN CHOPPED TOMATOES

1 TABLESPOON TOMATO PASTE (CONCENTRATED PUREE)

2 TABLESPOONS CHOPPED FLAT-LEAF PARSLEY

This is a nice huge amount – a good dishful that will give you plenty, even for next day. You can even freeze some portions. If this dish seems like too much work all in one go, you can make the meat sauce the day before. The wonderful thing that Roulla taught me here is to use olive oil instead of butter in the béchamel. Use a good-tasting olive oil, but you can still use butter if you prefer. I like this when the béchamel is like a duvet covering a bed of mince and fried eggplant and zucchini. Although it is known as a fairly heavy dish, you don't have to eat a huge portion.

Cut the eggplants lengthways into slices of about 5 mm (¼ inch). Sprinkle with salt and leave in a colander for ½ hour for the juices to drain. Slice the zucchini slightly thinner, also lengthways.

To make the meat sauce, heat the oil in a large non-stick frying pan, which has a lid. Add both minces and onion and fry until lightly brown and the moisture has gone. Add the garlic, cloves and allspice and when that smells good, add the wine. Simmer until most of it has evaporated. Add the tomatoes, tomato paste and parsley. Season well with salt and pepper. Stir in a tomato tin of water. Put the lid on and simmer for 1 hour, taking the lid off in the last 10 minutes if it looks liquidy (it needs to be fairly dry for the moussaka). Remove the cloves and allspice if you find them, then taste for seasoning.

Meanwhile, fry the eggplant and zucchini. Rinse the eggplants and dry them very well with paper towels. Heat very little olive oil in a large non-stick pan and fry the eggplant slices in batches. When the fried side is golden, flip the slices over and prick with a fork, especially where they may still be hard. Press the slices with the fork and they will soften some more. When they are golden, remove to a plate lined with a couple of layers of paper towels and sprinkle with salt. Continue until all the eggplant are done, adding as little olive oil to the pan as necessary. Fry the zucchini in the same way.

For the béchamel, heat the milk with the cinnamon and cloves in a saucepan and keep warm. Heat the oil in a large wide pot on low heat. Stir the flour in with a wooden spoon and continue stirring until smooth to cook it a bit. Add the warm milk bit by bit, stirring with the wooden spoon at first then changing to a whisk to give you a lump-free, thick béchamel (it's important that it's thick and glooping on the surface). Remove from the heat. Break the eggs into a bowl and whisk well. Add a good ladleful of béchamel to acclimatise

them, then whisk the lot back into the béchamel. Add the mizithra and whisk to incorporate. Add a good grind of pepper and taste for salt.

Preheat the oven to 180°c (350°f/gas 4). Layer the eggplant on the bottom of a 34 x 26 cm (13½ x 10½ inch) ovenproof dish, leaving no gaps. Layer the zucchini on top. Scrape the meat sauce over the vegetables, patting it down and smoothing the top to make a firm mattress for the béchamel to lie on. Spoon the béchamel on top and level the surface. Bake for 30 to 40 minutes or until the béchamel is firm and golden. Allow to cool and set for about 45 minutes before cutting. If you try to serve it earlier, it may not hold its shape and may ooze.

BÉCHAMEL

2 LITRES (70 FL OZ/8 CUPS) MILK

½ TEASPOON CINNAMON

¼ TEASPOON GROUND CLOVES

250 ML (9 FL OZ/1 CUP) OLIVE OIL

250 G (9 OZ/1⅔ CUPS) PLAIN (ALL-PURPOSE) FLOUR

80 G (2¾ OZ) MIZITHRA OR HARD SALTED RICOTTA, COARSELY GRATED

3 EGGS

TOMATES YEMISTES STUFFED TOMATOES

Ντομάτες γεμιστές

MAKES 12

12 LOVELY RIPE TOMATOES (ABOUT 160 G/5¾ OZ EACH)

250 ML (9 FL OZ/1 CUP) TOMATO PASSATA (PURÉED TOMATOES)

1 TEASPOON SUGAR

10 TABLESPOONS OLIVE OIL

140 G (5 OZ) ROUND SPRING ONIONS WITH SOME GREEN, CHOPPED

40 G (1½ OZ) CELERY WITH LEAVES, CHOPPED

2 GARLIC CLOVES, CHOPPED

120 G (4¼ OZ) MEDIUM-GRAIN RICE

3 TABLESPOONS COARSELY CHOPPED FLAT-LEAF PARSLEY

600 G (1 LB 5 OZ) POTATOES, PEELED, HALVED LENGTHWAYS, EACH HALF CUT INTO 3 OR 4 GONDOLAS

20 G (¾ OZ) BUTTER

This is often done with a mixture of different vegetables such as large zucchini and peppers. Here I have done only tomatoes. You may need to adjust cooking times or water amounts, as it will depend entirely on the tomatoes, but you need to cook this until there is only some thickened gooey liquid at the bottom of the dish and the tomatoes are tender and roasty but not falling apart, and the potatoes soft. I use a big round oven dish of about 34 cm (13½ inches). The tomatoes are lovely served with a dollop of Yoghurt on the side (page 131 with or without the mint and paprika) and a green salad on the side.

Top the tomatoes, keeping their hats aside for now. Scoop out the insides using a sharp knife and a sharp spoon. Take care not to pierce the shells. Put the pulp into a food processor or blender and pulse it to a thick juice. To this add the passata, sugar and a little salt and pepper, and mix in.

Preheat the oven to 170°c (325°f/gas 3). Heat 5 tablespoons of the olive oil in a medium pan and sauté the onion until softened. Add the celery and sauté on low heat until it is soft. Add the garlic and when that smells good, add 500 ml (17 fl oz/2 cups) of the tomato mixture. Bring to the boil then stir the rice in. Add enough water, 60–125 ml (2–4 fl oz/¼–½ cup), to prevent the mixture sticking. Cook for about 7 to 8 minutes. Remove from the heat and stir in the parsley.

Sprinkle the cavity of the tomatoes with a little salt. Fill each one two-thirds full with the rice mixture and put their hats on. Arrange the tomatoes in an ovenproof dish large enough to take them with the potatoes. Scatter the potatoes around, propping up any leaning tomatoes if necessary, and pour the remaining tomato juice over here and there. Drizzle the rest of the olive oil over the top of the tomatoes and sprinkle salt on the potatoes as well as on the tops of the tomatoes (some people like to sprinkle a little sugar on here, too). Dot the butter on the tomatoes and finally, pour 250 ml (9 fl oz / 1 cup) of water gently around the potatoes. Bake for about 1½ hours, turning the potatoes over and basting 3 or 4 times. Add a little more water if the sauce becomes too dry during this time, but this will depend entirely on your tomatoes. The finished dish should have some thickened sauce on the bottom.

PAPOUTSAKIA
SMALL SHOES

Παπουτσάκια

SERVES 8

4 LONG EGGPLANTS
(AUBERGINES, ABOUT
250 G/9 OZ EACH), ALL OF
THE SAME DIMENSIONS

ABOUT 125 ML (4 FL OZ/
½ CUP) OLIVE OIL, FOR
FRYING

1 LARGE RED ONION,
CHOPPED

400 G (14 OZ) MINCED BEEF

2 GARLIC CLOVES, FINELY
CHOPPED

125 ML (4 FL OZ/½ CUP)
RED WINE

2 X 400 G (14 OZ) TINS
CRUSHED TOMATOES

4 TABLESPOONS CHOPPED
FLAT-LEAF PARSLEY

BÉCHAMEL

40 G (1½ OZ) BUTTER

40 G (1½ OZ) PLAIN
(ALL-PURPOSE) FLOUR

300 ML (10½ FL OZ) MILK,
HEATED

A BIG PINCH OF NUTMEG

3 TABLESPOONS GRATED
KEFALOTIRI

These are basically the same ingredients as moussaka, but prepared differently and served in individual shoe servings.

Cut the eggplants in half lengthways, sprinkle the cut sides with salt and leave them upside-down in a colander for half an hour or so to drain away any bitter juices. Drizzle some oil into a large non-stick frying pan and when hot, add half the eggplant halves. Fry until deep golden and soft on both sides, and when you prick the thickest part with a fork there is no resistance. Remove to a platter and fry the remaining eggplant halves. When cooled, scoop out the flesh using a sharp spoon, leaving a 6 to 8 mm (¼ to ⅜ inch) border. Chop the flesh and put aside. Wipe out the frying pan with paper towels. Add 3 tablespoons of olive oil to it and sauté the onion until golden. Add the mince and fry until browned. Add the garlic, cook for a moment more until it smells good, then add the wine and let it simmer for a minute or two. Add 1 tin of tomatoes and the parsley, and season with salt and pepper. Cook, stirring a couple of times, for about 20 minutes or until thickened. Add the chopped eggplant and simmer for another 10 or 12 minutes or until most of the liquid has gone.

Preheat the oven to 180°c (350°f/gas 4). To make the béchamel, melt the butter in a heavy-

based saucepan over low heat and stir in the flour. Whisk the milk in gradually to ensure no lumps. Add the nutmeg and season with salt and a little pepper. Whisk until thick.

Empty the remaining tin of tomatoes over the bottom of a 26 x 34 cm (10½ x 13½ inch) roasting dish and add a little salt. Line up the eggplant shells on top, cut side up, and sprinkle with salt. Divide the mince mixture among them. Dollop 2 to 3 tablespoons of béchamel on each, scatter some kefalotiri over and pour 125 ml (4 fl oz / ½ cup) of water around them. Bake until roasty and golden on top, about 30 minutes.

LAHANODOLMADES CABBAGE ROLLS

Λαχανοντολμάδες

MAKES ABOUT 21

1 LARGE (ABOUT 1.6 KG/3 LB 8 OZ) SAVOY CABBAGE

200 G (7 OZ) MINCED PORK

200 G (7 OZ) MINCED BEEF

200 G (7 OZ) MEDIUM-GRAIN RICE

1 LARGE RED ONION, GRATED ON THE LARGE HOLES OF A GRATER

400 G (14 OZ) TIN CRUSHED TOMATOES

4 TABLESPOONS CHOPPED FLAT-LEAF PARSLEY

1 TEASPOON SWEET PAPRIKA

4 LEMONS

40 G (1½ OZ) UNSALTED BUTTER

4 TABLESPOONS OLIVE OIL

4 EGGS

This is wonderful. Although it may seem complicated it's quite straightforward. You will need a big and wide pot to hold the bundles, and a plate inverted into the pot to hold the bundles in place.

It's difficult to judge the exact amount of cabbage and filling here, it depends on how many untorn leaves you get from your cabbage. If you happen to end up with some spare filling, you can cook it on the stovetop with some water as an extra side. I love the savoy cabbage but you can use any type with big flat leaves.

This is not a dish that keeps very well as the sauce makes it difficult to warm up, so if you think this makes more than you'll need at one sitting, halve the recipe.

Carefully remove the cabbage leaves one by one with a small sharp knife, taking care not to break them. Rinse in cold water then boil in a large pot of boiling salted water in batches for just a few minutes until softened. Gently remove the leaves and put the cooking water aside for later. Don't discard the tough outer leaves or torn ones because they will be used later to line the cooking pot, and the smaller inner leaves can be used for any patching up. You will need about 21 good leaves. Rinse these under cold water, shake off the excess then lay them flat on trays lined with clean tea towels. Cut away any thick bottom stems if they look like they won't roll up easily.

In a bowl, mix together the minces, rice (uncooked), onion, tomato, parsley, paprika and juice of 1 lemon, and season well with salt and a few good grinds of pepper. Spoon a healthy wooden-spoonful (about 50 g/1¾ oz) of mixture onto the lower middle of the leaves. Start rolling up the filling from the bottom. Make one full turn, tuck both sides towards the middle then carry on rolling. Don't roll too tightly as the rice will expand during cooking, but they must be compact to hold their bundles.

Heat half the butter and half the oil in a large wide non-stick pot that has a lid. Line the bottom with the reserved outer cabbage leaves. Arrange the cabbage rolls tightly on top in concentric circles, starting from the outside. When one layer is full, make another on top until all the rolls are in. Dot the rest of the butter on top and drizzle the remaining oil over. Sprinkle lightly with salt and pepper. Pour in enough of the reserved cabbage water to just cover, about 750 ml (26 fl oz/3 cups). Find a plate which fits into the pot snugly and put it on top, inverted, to keep the bundles from moving about. Cover, bring gently to the boil and simmer for about 40 minutes or until the rolls are tender and the rice is

cooked. Add 1½ cups of water a few minutes before the end of cooking as you will need it for the sauce.

Whisk the eggs, the juice of the remaining 3 lemons and a little salt and pepper in a bowl. Whisk in about a cup of the hot cooking liquid to acclimatise the egg, remove the pot from the heat then pour the lot back into the pot. Distribute it by rocking the pot well. Return the pot to the lowest heat, shaking and rocking it until the sauce thickens a little. Be careful not to overheat it, as the eggs will scramble. If it doesn't look saucy enough, add a little hot water. Remove from the heat and rest it, covered, for a few minutes, rocking the pot now and then. Serve the rolls hot or warm, drizzled with a good amount of sauce, a light sprinkling of salt if necessary and a grinding of pepper.

KOKKINISTO REDDENED

Kokkινιστó

SERVES 6

6 TABLESPOONS OLIVE OIL

6 X 250 G (9 OZ) SLICES BEEF FOR STEWING (EG CHUCK, BLADE OR SHIN) ABOUT 3 CM (1¼ INCHES) THICK

1 LARGE RED ONION, CHOPPED

125 ML (4 FL OZ/½ CUP) RED WINE

400 G (14 OZ) TIN CRUSHED TOMATOES

1 TABLESPOON TOMATO PASTE (CONCENTRATED PUREE)

½ TEASPOON GROUND CINNAMON

2 TABLESPOONS CHOPPED FLAT-LEAF PARSLEY

3 THYME SPRIGS

This is called reddened because, quite simply, the meat is cooked in a tomato sauce. Simple meat stews like this with tomato, and the lemonato on the opposite page are very popular standard food in Greece. They would be served with some pasta on the side, or with chips, which is how I love it.

The chips in Greece often get an unusual sprinkling of cheese, which is wonderful and casual.

Preheat the oven to 180°c (350°f/gas 4). Heat 3 tablespoons of olive oil in a large non-stick frying pan and fry the beef until deep golden on both sides. Salt each side as it's done. Remove to a large cast-iron pot which has a lid. Add the rest of the olive oil and the onion to a pan and sauté it until softened.

Add the wine and cook until it has almost evaporated. Add the crushed tomato and the paste, the cinnamon and parsley, and season with a little salt and black pepper. Bring to the boil and simmer for a few minutes, squashing any big bits of tomato with a wooden spoon. Scrape out over beef. Fill the tomato tin with water and add this to the pot. Add the thyme, cover with the lid and bake for about 2 hours, turning the meat a couple of times. Add an extra 125 ml (4 fl oz/½ cup) of water, then bake for 30 minutes more. At the end of this time the beef should be very tender and the sauce thick and jammy, but abundant. If necessary, add a little hot water towards the end. Remove from the oven and serve.

LEMONATO LEMONED

Λεμονάτο

SERVES 6 OR SO

2 TABLESPOONS OLIVE OIL

40 G (1½ OZ) BUTTER

950 G (2 LB 2 OZ) VEAL NUT, TIED UP WITH STRING TO HOLD ITS SHAPE WHILE COOKING

1 GARLIC CLOVE, PEELED

½ SMALL ONION

JUICE OF 1 LARGE LEMON

You can use beef here and cook it in thick slices like the previous tomato version if you prefer. This is best for me with chips that can be dipped into the sauce too, but also wonderful with pasta.

Heat the oil and butter in a not too big cast-iron casserole, or a non-stick pot in which the meat will fit compactly. Brown the veal, sprinkling the done side with salt and pepper as you go. Add the garlic and onion, sauté to lightly golden for a moment, then add 250 ml (9 fl oz / 1 cup) of water and put the lid on. Simmer over very low heat for about 2 hours, turning it over a few times and adding 125 ml (4 fl oz / ½ cup) of water and the lemon juice 15 minutes before the end. It should be soft with a good amount of lemony sauce – add a little extra water if needed. Remove the onion and garlic. Take off the heat and rest in the pot, still covered, for 10 minutes before slicing and serving.

TIS ORAS

THERE + THEN FOODS

How-to-order in Greece: Once you have taken your table in a taverna – say on the beach – you could flip flop your way inside to see the food. After choosing a few mezedes for the middle of the table to start with, as a main you could choose between the ready-cooked foods on display or the 'there and then' foods, which are mostly grilled (or some fried) foods. These are often on display raw – and include fish, meat skewers etc. You can usually just indicate to a dish saying: 'parakalo' (please).

PSARI LADOLEMONO GRILLED FISH WITH LEMON OIL

Ψάρι λαδολέμονο

SERVES 4

4 TABLESPOONS OF
BEST OLIVE OIL

JUICE OF 1 LARGE
JUICY LEMON

1 GARLIC CLOVE

2 SEA BREAM (ABOUT
500 G/1 LB 2 OZ) EACH,
SCALED AND CLEANED

OLIVE OIL, FOR BRUSHING

ALATOPIPERIGANO
(PAGE 128), TO SERVE

2 TABLESPOONS ROUGHLY
CHOPPED FLAT-LEAF
PARSLEY, TO SERVE

This is the kind of thing to order on a Greek beach. It is extremely simple and good served with a dish of olives, some capers and some boiled vegetables dressed with olive oil on the side.

For grilling fish whole, it is good to have a double-sided grill rack so that you can just flip over the fish. This dish is also fantastic when done in the oven; salt and pepper the fish and roast it in a roasting dish with a couple of tablespoons of olive oil at 200°c (400°f / gas 6). Half an hour for a fish of this size should take it to ready. Then make the lemon oil, pour over the fish, rock the dish and serve.

Make the lemon oil by whipping the olive oil and lemon juice together in a small bowl until creamy. Add the whole garlic clove and put aside for the flavours to steep.

Rinse the fish inside and out, and cut off their fins. Pat them dry with paper towels. Scatter their insides with salt, and salt and lightly pepper their outer skin.

Preheat a barbecue grill to hot. Position the rack about 10 cm (4 inches) from the coals and brush it with olive oil. Lay the fish on top and grill until the underside is golden and crusty here and there. Turn them over and grill the other side too. Remove to a platter. Take the garlic clove out of the lemon oil and give it a final whip before drizzling over the fish. Scatter well with alatopiperigano then a nice sprinkling of parsley. Serve hot, with an extra bowl for the bones.

BARBOUNIA TIGANITA FRIED RED MULLET

Μπαρμπούνια τηγανιτά

SERVES 4

8 BARBOUNIA (RED MULLETS), ABOUT 80 G (2¾ OZ) EACH AND JUST UNDER 20 CM (8 INCHES) LONG, CLEANED, SCALED AND GUTTED

ABOUT 2 TABLESPOONS RED WINE VINEGAR

FLOUR, FOR DUSTING

LIGHT OLIVE OIL, FOR FRYING

LEMON QUARTERS, FOR SERVING

This simple dish of fried fish served with lemon is much loved in Greece. It would be ideal eaten looking out at the sea, but in any setting is very good. Nice served with a salad and horta.

Rinse the fish and pat dry with paper towels. Cut off the fins. Put the fish into a wide colander and splash well on both sides with the vinegar, then leave them for a few minutes. Put the flour in a large deep plate and stir through some salt and a few grinds of black pepper. Fill a deep bowl with cold water.

Pat each fish in the flour, coating both sides. Now quickly dip them in the cold water, shake, and pat them all over in flour once again.

Pour oil into a large frying pan to a depth of 1.5 to 2 cm (⅝ to ¾ inch) and put over a high heat. Fry the fish, turning them once, until crisp and golden on both sides. If they don't all fit, do them in 2 batches. Remove to a plate lined with paper towels. Serve hot with a sprinkling of salt, the lemons and a plate for the bones.

MARIDA/ATHERINA TIGANITI FRIED TINY FISH

Μαρίδα/Αθερίνα τηγανιτή

SERVES A COUPLE

A COUPLE OF HANDFULS
OF TINY FISH SUCH AS
WHITEBAIT OR SMELT

FLOUR, FOR DUSTING

LIGHT OLIVE OIL,
FOR FRYING

LEMON QUARTERS,
FOR SERVING

These are fried until crisp and eaten whole, like chips. You can use whitebait or any other tiny fish that can be eaten whole.

Rinse the fish and pat them dry on paper towels. Put some flour in a wide shallow bowl and season the flour with some salt and a few grinds of pepper.

Pour olive oil into a frying pan to a depth of 2 to 3 cm (¾ to 1¼ inches) and put over a high heat. Working in a couple of batches, toss the fish in the flour to coat, then fry them until crispy golden, turning them with a slotted spoon to ensure even frying. Remove to a plate lined with paper towels and sprinkle with a little salt as soon as they are all done. Serve with lemon for whoever wants.

KOLIOS (YOUNA) SUN-DRIED MACKEREL

Γούνα (κολιός)

SERVES 4

4 MACKEREL (ABOUT 300 G /10½ OZ EACH), CLEANED

ABOUT 2 TEASPOONS SALT

1 HEAPED TEASPOON DRIED OREGANO

OLIVE OIL, TO SERVE

LEMON QUARTERS, TO SERVE

My friend Kimon told me about this recipe first. I was intrigued, then found it on the island of Naxos with a potato salad that I have also given the recipe for (page 225). This fish is wonderful, unusual and very easy. It has a deep and honest flavour. It also goes well with something simple such as boiled zucchini (courgettes) and a lettuce and dill salad. Start with taramosalata, koulouria and maybe a dish of vinegared octopus.

Of course, this should only be done on a sunny day, and the amount of time the mackerel will need in the sun will depend on the strength of the sun. When salting fish, note that you need enough salt to dry as well as flavour it, but too much will ruin the flavour.

Cut the heads off the fish (or better, get your fishmonger to do it), slit through the belly and remove the innards. Gently open them out, leaving the spine in place on one side with the tail. Pick out any bones from the spineless half, rinse and pat dry with paper towels. Sprinkle both sides generously with salt (roughly ¼ teaspoon on each side – each fish gets ½ teaspoon of salt) and a few grinds of pepper and lay the fish on a tray, skin side down. Crumble the oregano over and cover with a cake net to keep insects away. Put out to dry in full sun for 5 to 6 hours, depending on the strength of the sun. Check now and then that they are drying but not shrivelling up.

Preheat the barbecue to very hot. Brush the grill with a little oil and add the fish skin side down, 8 to 10 cm (3¼ to 4 inches) from the coals. Grill until the skin is nice and crusty, then carefully turn the fish and grill just long enough for it to be gold here and there, but not dried out. Serve with a drizzle of olive oil and a good squeeze of lemon juice.

SOUVLAKI SE KALAMAKI PORK SKEWERS

Σουβλάκι (σε καλαμάκι)

MAKES ABOUT 12
SKEWERS

WOODEN SKEWERS
(KALAMAKI)

1.2 KG (2 LB 10 OZ) LEAN
PORK WITH SOME FAT

2 TEASPOONS DRIED
OREGANO

3 TABLESPOONS
OLIVE OIL

ABOUT 12 SLICES
COUNTRY BREAD,
ABOUT 2 CM (¾ INCH)
THICK, HALVED IF LARGE

ABOUT 2 LEMONS,
QUARTERED

These can either be wrapped in pita with tzatziki, tomatoes, lemon and parsley, as in the kebabs (page 288), or served as is on the stick with some grilled bread. Here then, extra oregano and salt should be scattered on and lemon wedges served on the side.

Use a part of the pork towards the shoulder where it's more tender. Pork fillets also work very well, just make sure you don't dry out the meat in the grilling as they have little fat.

Soak the skewers in cold water for about 30 minutes so they won't burn when they go over the coals. Trim any drastic fat off the pork but leave some on for flavour and moistness. Cut the meat into rough 2 cm (¾ inch) cubes. Thread 6 pork cubes onto each skewer, leaving space at the top to spike the bread.

Put the skewers onto a plate, sprinkle with the oregano that you crush between your fingers, a little salt, and pepper. Drizzle the oil over and turn to coat evenly.

Preheat the barbecue to high and put the rack about 10 cm (4 inches) from the coals. Grill the souvlaki until nice and grilled–looking here and there and still moist, not dry inside. Grill the bread lightly on both sides and spike it on the end of the skewers. Serve on a plate, or on squares of baking paper, scattering over some extra salt and crushing some oregano on. Serve hot, with lemon juice squeezed over.

KEBAB

Κεμπάπ

SERVES 4

250 G (9 OZ) FINELY GROUND LAMB MINCE

250 G (9 OZ) FINELY GROUND BEEF MINCE

1 SMALL RED ONION, GRATED

2 TABLESPOONS COARSELY CHOPPED FLAT-LEAF PARSLEY

½ TEASPOON DRIED OREGANO, CRUMBLED

11 THICK METAL SKEWERS

3 TOMATOES (ABOUT 120 G /4¼ OZ EACH), QUARTERED

OLIVE OIL, FOR BRUSHING

8 PITA BREAD, BOUGHT, OR (PAGE 158)

1 SMALL RED ONION (ABOUT 80 G/2¾ OZ), SLICED

A COUPLE OF HANDFULS COARSELY CHOPPED FLAT-LEAF PARSLEY

TZATZIKI (PAGE 130), TO SERVE

LEMON QUARTERS, TO SERVE

PAPRIKA IN A SHAKER, TO SERVE

8 SQUARES BAKING PAPER, ROUGHLY 25 CM (10 INCHES)

There are foods which are taken from neighbouring countries and immigration that then become a fixed item, such as kebabs, which have Turkish origins.

The mince here should have a little fat and the kebabs must be cooked over very hot coals so that they are nicely charred but still moist inside. If you don't have the skewers, you can just pat the meat into sausage shapes and grill anyway. Eating two of these in pita is not unreasonable if you are not having anything else?

The thing about eating these is that the warm juice runs the length of the meat into the pita, like a small stream in a current, and pools in the bottom, dripping inevitably through the soaked paper onto your hand. So you will need some aeroplane-like wet towels – or simply apologise to the next batch of people you are introduced to or run into and have to kiss on both cheeks.

Put the minces, grated onion, parsley and oregano in a bowl and add ¾ to 1 teaspoon salt. Knead together thoroughly. Divide into 8 balls of about 80 g (2¾ oz) each. Firmly press each ball compactly around a skewer in a long sausage shape of about 15 cm (6 inches) long. Thread 4 tomato quarters on each of the remaining skewers, making sure that you pierce through the skin so that they hold well.

Preheat the grill to high and brush it lightly with olive oil. Grill the meat kebabs until deep gold and slightly crusty in parts on the outside and still moist on the inside, but not dried out. Brush the tomatoes with a little olive oil, scatter lightly with salt and pepper and grill them at the same time. Brush the pita very lightly with olive oil on both sides (or leave plain if you prefer) and put on the grill to warm up.

To serve, remove the skewers from the kebabs. Halve the tomato quarters. Put a square of baking paper on each plate and then 1 pita on top of each of these. Add a meat kebab, a couple of pieces of tomato, some onion slices, a good amount of parsley, a nice dab of tzatziki, a squeeze of lemon juice and a shaking of paprika. Add salt if you like. Roll up the pita quite tightly then roll the paper around. Tuck the bottom in and leave the top third of the pita out. Eat. Move on to your second one. Then follow with a nice ice cream.

Greek (dried) oregano has a deep, intense and yet not overpowering flavour. I like to think that while these herbs are growing, they must somehow capture the mountains, sea, ambience and Greek love in their growth, in their leaves. And then they are pulled from the earth, dried up in bundles in our homes, for all of the above to be unleashed into our pots and on our food when the oregano lands. So use Greek oregano if possible.

BIFTEKIA GRILLED BEEF BURGERS

Μπιφτέκια

MAKES 16

100 G (3½ OZ) CRUSTLESS
WHITE BREAD (4 SLICES)

1 KG (2 LB 4 OZ) MINCED
BEEF, WITH SOME FAT

1 EGG, LIGHTLY BEATEN

1 MEDIUM–LARGE RED
ONION, GRATED ON THE
LARGE HOLES OF A GRATER

3 HEAPED TABLESPOONS
ROUGHLY CHOPPED
FLAT-LEAF PARSLEY

1 TABLESPOON
CHOPPED MINT

1 RIPE TOMATO, GRATED
ON THE LARGE HOLES OF A
GRATER SO THE SKIN STAYS
BEHIND IN YOUR HAND

2 LEMONS, QUARTERED

These are definitely best grilled over charcoal, but you could also cook them in a chargrill (griddle) pan as a second option. They can be prepared beforehand and kept in the fridge, which is a great feeling, to open the fridge and find it all done when you're in that last-minute rush of getting everything together at once. I like to serve these with simple things, like the roast lemon potatoes, a tomato salad and bread.

Tear the bread into pieces and put in a bowl with about a cup of water. Soak for 10 minutes or so. Put the mince into a bowl and add the egg, onion, parsley, mint and tomato. Season well with salt and pepper. Squish the bread and squeeze out the excess water very well with your hands. If necessary press the bread in a sieve to make sure all the water is squeezed out. The mixture here is very soft, which is important for the end result, but the soaked bread must be very well squeezed out or the burgers won't hold their shape. Add the bread to the bowl. Mix it together, making sure everything is incorporated, then knead well to give a lovely soft mixture. Divide into 16 balls of about 90 g (3¼ oz) each. Shape into firm flat ovals of about 11 x 7 cm (4¼ x 2¾ inches) and put on a tray. Keep in the fridge while you get your barbecue heated to very hot (or if you won't be cooking them immediately).

Brush the barbecue grill very lightly with oil, then cook the burgers on the grill about 10 cm (4 inches) away from the coals, pressing them gently with an egg flip to keep their shape. When the undersides are deep golden, turn and do the other side. They should be crusty dark gold here and there but still moist inside. Sprinkle with a little salt and serve at once, with lemon quarters.

SWEET FOODS

As close up and alive and now as the Greeks may be ... there is an incredible feeling of past and tradition embroidered through their linens and laces. And a knowing that you could just turn up at someone's house for the first time and enter through the back door. It is a nation not styled and sitting pretty. Not one of those distant, unreachable races. But a lot of loud late celebrating nights, and sleeping-in, coffee-drinking, communicating tavli players who love their history and their country. Of uncles pinching your cheeks till they hurt. And aunts' large arms waiting to embrace you. Of desserts drenched with Greek love and syrup.

You may as well surrender.

KARPOUZI ME FETA WATERMELON + FETA

Καρπούζι με φέτα

1 WATERMELON

FETA

Not quite a dessert, more a Greek snack. On a hot summer's day to sit under a Greek tree at the end of a road or on a beach and see miles of endless sea, with watermelon, feta and a knife must be one of the greatest things in realising the spacings that exist in Greece. This is wonderful, sweet and salty. Great.

Cut off the rind then slice the watermelon flesh into chunks and put on a plate. Break the feta into chunks and eat with the watermelon. That's it.

IPOVRIHIO SUBMARINE

Υποβρύχιο

MAKES ABOUT 2 CUPS

620 G (1 LB 6 OZ) CASTER (SUPERFINE) SUGAR

1 VANILLA BEAN, SPLIT

1 TEASPOON LEMON JUICE

Old Greece. Love this. Greek children adore it. Very very sweet. Can be flavoured with vanilla, rose, pistachio, lemon, and probably other flavours as well. It's so sugary and thick that you scoop it up and it clings to the spoon. You submarine that into a glass of ice-cold water, then lick the water off the spoon and some of the ipovrihio comes off as well. And on you go until it's all finished. Some people even like to drink the water then. One spoonful of this would seem enough, but then, sometimes they come and ask for more.

You can buy it anywhere in Greece. Or you could try this at home.

Put the sugar in a saucepan with 7 tablespoons of water. Stir until the sugar dissolves, add the vanilla bean then bring to the boil. Simmer until thickened (when a blob of syrup dropped in a glass of cold water forms a soft ball, 112–116°c/234–241°f on a sugar thermometer). Add the lemon juice and continue to boil for a minute or two, then remove from the heat.

Strain it into a bowl and leave to cool to lukewarm. It will turn white as it cools. Stir with a wooden spoon in the same direction until it thickens. To serve, scoop a spoonful and dip it into a glass of ice-cold water. Keeps well in an airtight container.

✿ For rose ipovrihio, omit the vanilla bean and stir (in the same direction) through 2 teaspoons of rosewater and a few drops of red food colouring just before you start stirring.

YIAOURTI ME MELI GREEK YOGHURT, HONEY + NUTS

Γιαούρτι με μέλι

FOR ONE

2 DOLLOPS OF GREEK YOGHURT

1 HEAPED TABLESPOON BROKEN-UP SHELLED WALNUT HALVES

ABOUT 2 TEASPOONS THICK BUT DROP-OFF-THE-SPOON HONEY

GROUND CINNAMON, FOR SCATTERING

A fresh fruit cut up over this is also lovely. The nuts are nice lightly toasted in a dry frying pan, but you may be having this on an island somewhere and not have your frying pan with you. This is a lovely breakfast.

Dollop yoghurt into a bowl. Sprinkle with walnuts, scatter on a little cinnamon, drizzle over some honey and give a final scattering of cinnamon.

GLIKO TOU KOUTALIOU SPOON SWEETS

Γλυκό του κουταλιού

SERVES 9 TO 12

CHERRY SPOON SWEETS

500 G (1 LB 2 OZ) SUGAR

500 G (1 LB 2 OZ) LARGE SOUR OR UNDER-RIPE CHERRIES

1 STRIP LEMON ZEST

1 TABLESPOON ALMOND OR CHERRY LIQUEUR

CHESTNUT SPOON SWEETS

500 G (1 LB 2 OZ) FRESH CHESTNUTS, SHELL ON

500 G (1 LB 2 OZ) SUGAR

1 TABLESPOON HONEY

1 TABLESPOON LEMON JUICE

There are many varieties of this very typical sweet: sour cherry, lemon blossom, rose petal, green walnut, chestnut, watermelon rind, fig, quince, baby clementine, apricot, grapes ... They are really lovely looking, lying in a thick syrup bath. You may be offered one when you visit someone, always with a glass of ice-cold water. The fruit pieces should not be too big, just large enough to fit on a small spoon which you would dip (only once of course) into the jar. Serve another spoon if people want more, but normally just one gives you enough of the sweetness you need.

For the cherry spoon sweets,
put the sugar in a large pan with 250 ml (9 fl oz/1 cup) of water and stir until the sugar dissolves. Wash the cherries well and remove the stems. Pit them then stir into the sugar and water. Leave to steep for 3 hours. Add the lemon zest and liqueur. Without stirring, bring to the boil over high heat. Simmer for 5 to 6 minutes, skimming the surface with a slotted spoon as necessary. Remove the cherries to a sterilised preserving jar and continue cooking the syrup until it is very thick – 110°c (230°f) on a sugar thermometer if you have one. Cool a little before pouring over the cherries and sealing.

For the chestnut spoon sweets,
prepare the chestnuts by cutting a cross in the shell of each one with a small sharp knife, being careful not to cut into the flesh. Bring a large pot of water to the boil and add half the chestnuts. Simmer for 5 minutes then scoop out with a slotted spoon. Cool for a minute or two then gently peel off the shell. Repeat with the remaining chestnuts. Now put them all in a pot, cover with cold water and bring to the boil. Simmer until

their skins loosen, just a few minutes, then drain. While still hot, gently rub them in a tea towel to remove the skins still attached to the nut.

Put the sugar, honey and lemon juice in a pan with 250 ml (9 fl oz / 1 cup) of water and stir over medium heat until sugar dissolves. Add the chestnuts and bring to the boil. Simmer for 7 to 8 minutes. Remove the chestnuts with a slotted spoon to a sterilised preserving jar and continue cooking the syrup until it thickens, 110°c (230°f) on a sugar thermometer. Cool a little before pouring over the chestnuts and sealing.

For the quince spoon sweets,

Peel, quarter and core the quinces. Cut the quarters into thick slices, large enough to fit on a dessert spoon. Put in a pot with 2 litres of water and bring to the boil. Simmer, covered, until the quinces turn a lovely gold-red, from 2 to 3 hours depending on how ripe your quinces are. Check the water level from time to time and top it up if necessary.

Put the sugar and 1 cup of the quince water in another pot and stir until the sugar dissolves. Using a slotted spoon, transfer the quince slices to the new pot and add the vanilla, cinnamon and lemon juice. Bring to the boil and simmer for 8 to 10 minutes. Remove the quinces with the slotted spoon and put into a sterilised preserving jar. Continue cooking the syrup until it thickens, 110°c (230°f) on a sugar thermometer if you have one. Cool a little before pouring over the quinces and sealing.

For the fig spoon sweets,

put the sugar and honey in a large pan with 250 ml (9 fl oz / 1 cup) and stir until the sugar dissolves. Add the figs, cinnamon

QUINCE SPOON SWEETS

3 QUINCES

500 G (1LB 2 OZ) SUGAR

1 VANILLA BEAN, SPLIT

1 CINNAMON ROLL

2 TEASPOONS LEMON JUICE

FIG SPOON SWEETS

500 G (1 LB 2 OZ) SUGAR

1 TABLESPOON HONEY

500 G (1 LB 2 OZ) FIRM UNDER-RIPE FIGS

1 CINNAMON ROLL

1 SMALL STRIP LEMON ZEST

---

continued

and lemon zest. Without stirring, bring to the boil then simmer for about 8 minutes. Remove the figs gently with a slotted spoon and put them in a shallow bowl which will take them in a single layer. Continue cooking the syrup until it thickens, 110°c (230°f) on a sugar thermometer if you have one. Cool a little before pouring over the figs. Cool completely before putting in a sterilised preserving jar and sealing.

ME PIRE O IPNOS – SLEEP TOOK ME
(AND CARRIED ME FAR AWAY ...)

To sterilise the jars, lay a thick layer of newspaper or tea towels on one or 2 oven shelves (being careful to avoid the flame if using a gas oven) and preheat the oven to 180°c (350°f/gas 4). Arrange the cleaned jars, opened end up, and their lids on the shelves. Close the oven door and heat for 18–20 minutes. Using thick pot holders, remove each jar from the oven as needed and put on a thick layer of newspaper to fill. Avoid putting a hot jar on a cold surface. The oven temperature can be dropped to 150°c/300°f/gas 2) to hold the jars until you are ready to fill each one with hot food. If you are putting cold food in, it must go into cold jars.

KRASSOKOULOURA WINE RINGS

Красокоύλоура

MAKES ABOUT 20

300 G (10½ OZ/2 CUPS) PLAIN (ALL-PURPOSE) FLOUR

1 TEASPOON BAKING POWDER

100 G (3½ OZ) SUGAR

1 TEASPOON GROUND CINNAMON

¼ TEASPOON GROUND CLOVES

90 ML (3 FL OZ) OLIVE OIL

125 ML (4 FL OZ/½ CUP) WHITE WINE

Greece is full of koulouria and koulourakia (this is the much used diminutive in Greek). Sweet and savoury, there are many different varieties of these round biscuits. Vanilla, citrus, sesame, cinnamon are some others you may come across. These ones are with wine. They will last for quite a while in a tin.

Preheat the oven to 180°c (350°f/gas 4). Put the flour, baking powder, sugar, cinnamon and cloves in a bowl and add a pinch of salt. Stir with a wooden spoon to combine, then stir in the olive oil and wine. Mix with your hands, adding a little more flour or wine as necessary to get a soft, uniform dough. Knead well for a couple of minutes.

Divide the dough into ovally balls of roughly 30 g (1 oz) each. Leave these at room temperature, uncovered, for about 5 minutes to rest the dough. Using your hands, roll each out into a rope 25 cm (10 inches) or so long. Join the ends and pat one end over the other to close the bracelet. Put as many as will fit onto a baking tray lined with baking paper and bake for about 20 to 25 minutes or until crisp and golden. Bake the rest.

LOUKOUMI ROSE DELIGHT

Λουκούμι

MAKES 28 PIECES

440 G (15½ OZ/2 CUPS) SUGAR

1 TEASPOON LEMON JUICE

60 G (2¼ OZ/½ CUP) CORNFLOUR

½ TEASPOON CREAM OF TARTAR

2 TEASPOONS ROSEWATER

20 G (¾ OZ) SHELLED PISTACHIOS, HALVED LENGTHWAYS

RED FOOD COLOURING

30 G (1 OZ/¼ CUP) ICING (CONFECTIONERS') SUGAR, FOR COATING

2 TABLESPOONS CORNFLOUR, EXTRA FOR COATING

These are most well known as Turkish delight. They are the sweets you are offered when you stop in at someone's even just for a quick visit. They are served with a glass of cold water. Loukoumia are also beautiful cut up into very small squares and served next to a coffee. The island of Syros is well known for their loukoumi. They are often flavoured with rose, mastiha or pistachio.

A sugar thermometer is important here to tell you when the sugar syrup is at the right stage.

Put the sugar and lemon juice in a pan with 185 ml (6 fl oz/¾ cup) of water. Stir until the sugar dissolves. Bring to the boil. Simmer without stirring for 30 or 40 minutes, or until a small dab is soft and pliable between your fingers when it's dropped into cold water (soft ball stage or 116°c/240°f on a sugar thermometer).

Combine the cornflour and cream of tartar in a heavy-based saucepan and whisk in 375 ml (13 fl oz/1½ cups) water until smooth. Cook on medium, stirring constantly, until thick. Slowly stir in the sugar syrup. Simmer over very low heat (or use a simmer mat) until very thick and pale golden, 60 to 70 minutes. Stir often to ensure that your mixture isn't sticking to the pan. Brush a 21 x 12 cm (8¼ x 4½ inch) dish with straight sides with oil and line with plastic wrap. Stir the rosewater and pistachios into the mixture and add the colouring drop by drop until you have a soft rose-petal pink. Pour into the dish and cool overnight, covered by a cake net.

Combine the icing sugar and cornflour on a plate. Cut the loukoumi into 3 cm (1¼ inch) squares and toss in the sugar mix. It will keep for weeks in a covered tin or box, not an airtight container.

YIAOURTOPITA YOGHURT CAKE

Γιαουρτόπιτα

MAKES 1 CAKE

180 G (6½ OZ) UNSALTED
BUTTER, ROOM
TEMPERATURE

250 G (9 OZ) SUGAR

3 EGGS

1 TEASPOON VANILLA
ESSENCE

300 G (10½ OZ/2 CUPS)
PLAIN (ALL-PURPOSE)
FLOUR

1 TABLESPOON BAKING
POWDER

250 G (9 OZ/1 CUP) GREEK
YOGHURT

I love this for its damp crumbs and great texture. It's the kind of cake that can be taken just about anywhere and it will be the right thing.

Preheat the oven to 180°c (350°f/gas 4) and butter and flour a 24 cm (9½ inch) spring-form tin. Beat the butter and sugar together with electric beaters until pale. Add the eggs one at a time, beating well after each addition. Add the vanilla and beat in well. Add the flour, baking powder and a pinch of salt together with the yoghurt, and beat until thick and smooth. Spoon into the tin.

Bake for about 45 minutes or until a skewer inserted into the centre comes out clean. The cake should be lovely and moist so be careful not to over-bake it. Check after about 30 minutes and cover the surface with foil if it is browning too quickly. Remove from the oven and cool in the tin for 10 to 15 minutes before turning out onto a wire cake rack.

MOUSTALEVRIA GRAPE JUICE PUDDING

Μουσταλευριά

MAKES ABOUT 15

1.25 KG (2 LB 12 OZ) SEEDLESS RED GRAPES, RINSED, DRAINED

1 TABLESPOON SUGAR

½ TEASPOON GROUND CINNAMON

35 G (1¼ OZ) CORNFLOUR

1 FLAT TABLESPOON SESAME SEEDS

You can make this from red or white grapes – muscats would be lovely. But the type of grapes you use are very important for the colour as well as the flavour. Here I have used uva fragola (concord/American) grapes, which give an amazing intensity of colour and taste.

The best way to extract the juice is to put them through a juicer, and bear in mind that you may need more or less grapes, depending on how much juice they have.

This can also be served in small bowls as a pudding, in which case use a little less cornflour. Moustalevria is traditionally a worker's food, given to those who help with the harvest, so it is most often eaten in September.

Blend the grapes in a blender or food processor until liquid and sieve out the skins, or pass them through a juicer. If you can't get seedless grapes, you will have to use a juicer. You will need 750 ml (26 fl oz/3 cups) of juice, so you can drink any left over. Put the juice into a pot, bring to the boil and simmer uncovered for about 15 minutes, skimming the surface of scum with a slotted spoon. Add the sugar and cinnamon halfway through. Put the cornflour into a cup and stir in 3 tablespoons of cold water, mixing it until smooth. Gradually stir this into the simmering grape juice. Whisk over low heat until it has thickened a lot to a creamy pudding, about 15 minutes. Scrape into a rectangular dish of roughly 18 cm x 13 cm (7 x 5 inches) and level the surface. Cool a little before scattering with the sesame seeds. Cool completely and refrigerate overnight before cutting into squares.

PAGOTO KAIMAKI SALEPI + MASTICHA ICE CREAM

Παγωτό καϊμάκι

SERVES 6 TO 8

½ TEASPOON MASTIC GRANULES

160 G (5¾ OZ) SUGAR

750 ML (26 FL OZ/3 CUPS) MILK

2 TEASPOONS GROUND SALEPI

185 ML (6 FL OZ/¾ CUP) POURING CREAM

This has a very definite, almost chewy texture that is instantly recognisable.

I went to a spice shop in the heart of Athens to buy the salepi (orchid root) needed, and the man spun around when I mentioned it, he was clearly happy that I would be making kaimaki and started thus to recite his recipe. He mimed and mimicked and gesticulated, rambling along his Greek road of youth. Hse explained, plucking his finger out of the imaginary 30 degrees milk that we would now be ready to stir in the rest. Then came the stirring motion of the wooden spoon and the electric beaters next, which were so realistically beating against the sides of the bowl with his clucking that I almost imagined that the ice cream would be appearing out of thin air any moment.

Grind the mastic with a little of the sugar to make dust. This is best done in a spice grinder but a mortar and pestle is fine too. Put the rest of the sugar in a pot with the milk and heat to just below boiling point. Take off the heat and whisk in the ground mastic and salepi, and keep whisking until they are all dissolved. Leave to cool. Whisk in the cream then pour into an ice-cream machine and freeze according to the manufacturer's instructions. Alternatively, pour into a shallow tray and put in the freezer. When it starts to set, beat it well with a fork to break up the ice crystals. Repeat this 3 or 4 more times until the ice cream is smooth and solid.

OUZO SORBET

Σορμπέ ούζου

SERVES 6 TO 8

220 G (7¾ OZ/1 CUP) SUGAR

7 TABLESPOONS OUZO

This is like a soft snow, sweet and ouzo-y and it works well after a meal – like an after-dinner mint

Stir the sugar into 750 ml (26 fl oz/3 cups) of water and bring to the boil. Simmer for 5 minutes. Cool. Stir in the ouzo and transfer to an ice-cream machine. Freeze following the manufacturer's instructions. Alternatively, pour into a shallow tray and put in the freezer, breaking it up and beating with a fork 3 or 4 times before it becomes solid.

KEIK PORTOKALI ORANGE SEMOLINA CAKE

Κέικ σιμιγδαλένιο με πορτοκάλι

MAKES ABOUT 24 DIAMONDS

2 ORGANIC ORANGES (EG NAVEL), WELL SCRUBBED

185 ML (6 FL OZ/¾ CUP) OLIVE OIL

140 G (5 OZ/²/₃ CUP) SUGAR

5 EGGS

250 G (9 OZ/2 CUPS) FINE SEMOLINA

4 TEASPOONS BAKING POWDER

80 G (2¾ OZ/½ CUP) ALMONDS, CHOPPED

SYRUP

125 G (4½ OZ) SUGAR

JUICE OF ¼ LEMON

1 TEASPOON ANTHONERO (FLOWER WATER EG LEMON OR ORANGE BLOSSOM, SEE GLOSSARY)

I got this recipe from my friend Artemis who in turn got it from her friend Galatia. They serve it with a Greek coffee. Sometimes with a scoop of ice cream on the side.

I have halved the syrup amount, but you decide after the first time whether you want to up the syrup again and make it more traditional, damper and sweeter.

Boil the whole oranges in plenty of water until softened, about 1 hour. Keep checking that they are well covered and add hot water as needed.

Preheat the oven to 180°c (350°f/gas 4). Oil and flour a 24 cm (9½ inch) cake tin (not spring-form). Put the syrup ingredients in a saucepan with 185 ml (6 fl oz/¾ cup) of water and stir over a medium-high heat until the sugar dissolves. Bring to the boil and simmer uncovered for 6 to 7 minutes. Set aside to cool.

Quarter the oranges to check that there are no pips. Puree them skin and all in a blender or food processor until you have a smooth orange mush. Pour this into a bowl and stir in the oil, sugar and eggs. Now whip with beaters, then beat in the semolina, baking powder and almonds. Scrape out into the cake tin and bake until a skewer inserted in the centre comes out clean, about 40 minutes. Cool the cake in the tin for 10 minutes or so. Still in the tin, cut it into diamonds about 7 cm (2¾ inches) long and 4 cm (1½ inches) across the middle. Gently pour the cooled syrup over the top, covering all the cake. Leave to cool completely before serving.

PASTELLI SESAME AND PISTACHIO SNACK

Παστέλι

MAKES ABOUT 30 SQUARES

125 G (4½ OZ) SESAME SEEDS

40 G (1½ OZ) SHELLED PISTACHIOS, BROKEN IN HALF

50 G (1¾ OZ) SUGAR

4 TABLESPOONS MILD RUNNY HONEY

A very good nutritious sweet snack. Kids love to eat this at a paniyiri (a local fair honouring saints). In the good old days it was seen as a good thing, an extravagance – 'finish your food and you can have a piece of pastelli'. I love it with pistachio nuts that the island of Aegina is so well known for.

It is very easy to make yourself, and the amount can easily be doubled. Keeps in an airtight container for many days.

Put the sesame seeds and pistachios into a non-stick frying pan and toast lightly to colour them. Keep aside. Add the sugar to the pan and cook, without stirring, over a low heat until it melts and becomes lightly golden. Standing back, add the honey. Stir in the sesame seeds and pistachios and mix while you can as it will be sticky and thick.

Scrape out onto a flat, heat-proof surface such as marble or a plastic pastry sheet, or even a large flat plate. Flatten it a bit with the back of a spoon then use your hands dipped in cold water to form a rectangular shape. Use a rolling pin to level the surface and to stretch the rectangle to roughly 15 x 18 cm (6 x 7 inches) and 5 mm (¼ inch) thick. Wait for a few minutes then cut into 3 cm (1¼ inch) squares (or rectangles). If you leave it standing too long it will become too hard to cut.

MELOPITA HONEY CAKE

Μελόπιτα

SERVES 8

2 EGGS

40 G (1½ OZ) SUGAR

2 TABLESPOONS PLAIN (ALL-PURPOSE) FLOUR

100 G (3½ OZ) HONEY

1 TABLESPOON LEMON JUICE

1 TABLESPOON BRANDY

500 G (1 LB 2 OZ) SOFT MIZITHRA OR RICOTTA CHEESE

1 TABLESPOON SUGAR, EXTRA

1 HEAPED TEASPOON GROUND CINNAMON

You will need a round ceramic dish of about 25 cm (10 inches). I love this served with figs, either fresh, or roasted with a little honey and sesame seeds. I have added a splash of brandy to the simple but lovely ingredients here.

Preheat the oven to 180°c (350°f/gas 4). Butter and flour an 25 cm (10 inch) ovenproof round ceramic dish. Put the eggs and sugar into a bowl and beat using electric beaters until voluminous, creamy and thick. Beat in the flour. Add the honey, lemon juice and brandy, and tip in the mizithra. Whisk well until it's thick, creamy and ribbony. Scrape into the baking dish and rock it to distribute evenly. Bake until a bit golden, about 30 minutes. Scatter the extra sugar and sieve the cinnamon over. Serve at room temperature or cover and refrigerate, as it is also good cold.

KAFES ELLINIKOS GREEK COFFEE

Ελληνικός Καφές

The muddy-on-the-bottom, thick and great-tasting coffee served in small cups is the kind you'll find the older generation in particular drinking. You need a small coffee pot (briki) which are available in different sizes. When ordering you will be asked how you want your coffee; glyki (sweet), metrio (medium) or sketo (no sugar). The sugar is stirred into the water with the ground coffee before heating. Before drinking it needs to sit for a minute so the sediment can fall to the bottom of the cup.

When you have finished your coffee, maybe you can find a Greek woman who knows about these things to read your cup for you. Or turn it upside down and let the coffee remains dribble down into the shapes that they will take. And then you can interpret interesting stories. A long line surely means a journey?

Fill your Greek coffee cup with room temperature water to more or less the level you want your coffee. Tip that into the briki and add 1 heaped teaspoonful of Greek coffee. Stir in 2 teaspoons of sugar for sweet (glyki), 1 teaspoon for medium (metrio), and no sugar is sketo. Put the briki over the flame and remove from the heat just before it reaches a rolling boil. Cool momentarily before repeating, not allowing it to boil as this can destroy the froth (kaimaki). (If your froth has bubbles in it, they say it must mean love — one way or another …)

Serve with a glass of cold water.

INDEX

INDEX

INDEX

INDEX

Acknowledgements

A big and humble thank you to all who helped me put this book together.

To my team: photographer Manos, stylist Michail and art director Lisa – thank you from the bottom of my heart. I would never make it to page 2 without you. A very big thank you to Jo and Luisa for all your wonderful and much-needed help.

Thank you Lisa M.G for all your support and encouragement always, and to all my friends at home for helping me in your various ways: thanks xx Anjalika, Mariella, Joan, Andrea, Rebecca, Peta, Anabelle, Scilla, Roberto, Leontine, Patrizia, Tanya, Balthazar, Didi, Corinne, Marion, Theo, Luciano and Stefania.

From my Greek side of things thank you all for your big contributions, I am always grateful:

thank you to my Greek angel helpers Anais, Danille and Katerina and to Artemis, Kyriakos, Christina, Galatia, Emily, Niko P, Roulla ... thank you to Ketty, Nikola, Uncle Makis, Niko T, Anette, Kiki, Iria, Irini, Katerina, Kimon, Maria, Ariana, Minnie, Mr. Angelos, Kiria Fotini, Virginia, Angela, Elpida, Leta, Elsa and Maria.

To my publisher, Kay, thank you for possibility. And to all at Murdoch – especially Daniela and Vivien – thank you for your support and everything that you have given the book.

To Mom, Dad, Nin and Ludi thank you, thank you, and to Santo Giovanni and Cassia and Yasmine – thank you for all that you are.

Tess x ♡ ♡